A Primer on Securitization

A Primer on Securitization

edited by Leon T. Kendall
and Michael J. Fishman

The MIT Press
Cambridge, Massachusetts
London, England

This book was set in Palatino by Wellington Graphics.
Printed on recycled paper and bound in the United States of America.

Library of Congress Cataloging-in-Publication Data

A Primer on securitization / edited by Leon T. Kendall and Michael J. Fishman.
    p. cm.
  Includes bibliographical references and index.
  ISBN 0-262-11211-6 (alk. paper)
  1. Asset-backed financing—Congresses. I. Kendall, Leon T.
II. Fishman, Michael J., 1957–   .
HG4028.A84P75 1996
658.15—dc20   95-53328
                                                                      CIP

Contents

Preface

There is little doubt that securitization is changing the face of mortgage, consumer, and corporate finance. Most new home mortgages and growing numbers of multifamily and commercial property mortgages are being funded by conversion into securities. Car loans and leases, credit card receivables, boat loans, mobile home loans, home equity loans, small business loans, student loans, problem loans, Third World debt, and even delinquent municipal tax liens also have been securitized by originators and Wall Street. Such financing is attracting the attention of an increasing number of corporate finance executives. It has important implications for banks, thrifts, and other intermediaries as they find themselves users of and competitors with securitization. Institutional investors competing for yield find themselves exposed to a whole new family of investment products, sometimes with troubling consequences. These are changing times in finance.

The chapters in this book were originally lectures delivered during an eight-week Colloquium on Securitization held at the Kellogg Graduate School of Management at Northwestern University in the spring of 1994. The Colloquium, cosponsored by Kellogg and Freddie Mac, brought together prominent finance professionals who qualify to be called the founders of securitization. In their fields, they constructed the foundations on which today's market rests and continues to build. Approximately 150 Kellogg students were joined by 60 members of the Chicago-area financial community in attending the Colloquium. This book is intended for those interested in the past, present, and future of asset-backed securities. The chapters assume that the reader has no detailed knowledge of securitization but does have a general knowledge of finance.

Financial support for the Colloquium from Freddie Mac is gratefully acknowledged. We thank Leland C. Brendsel, chairman and CEO of Freddie Mac, and Donald P. Jacobs, dean of the Kellogg Graduate

School of Management, for their joint vision of creating an academic/business partnership to explore this important topic in finance. John Gibbons, senior vice president, Corporate Relations and assistant to the chairman of Freddie Mac, Beth Preiss, principal economist of Freddie Mac, and Marc Landsberg, director of external relations of Kellogg also made essential contributions to the planning, development, and successful execution of the Colloquium. Caroline O'Kicki and Lolotte Olkowski of Kellogg made sure each week of the Colloquium went smoothly and efficiently. Finally, we thank Ann Sochi of The MIT Press for all of her help.

The views expressed in this book are not necessarily those of the Colloquium sponsors.

Contributors

Neil D. Baron, Vice Chairman and General Counsel
Fitch Investors Service

Steven P. Baum, Executive Vice President
Paine Webber

Leland C. Brendsel, Chairman and CEO
Freddie Mac

Lowell Bryan, Director
McKinsey & Co.

Dennis M. Cantwell, Vice President Corporate Finance and Development
Chrysler Financial Corporation

Laurence D. Fink, Chairman and CEO
Blackrock Financial Group

Robert D. Graffam, Director, Treasury Syndications and Financial Policy
International Finance Corporation

Michael Jungman, Vice President
J. P. Morgan & Co.

Leon T. Kendall, Professor of Finance and Real Estate
Kellogg Graduate School of Management, Northwestern University

Neil Kochen, Managing Director
Aetna Life Insurance and Annuity Co., Inc.

Mark L. Korell, President and CEO
GMAC Mortgage Corporation

Marcia Myerberg, Chief Executive
Myerberg & Company, L. P.

Susan M. Phillips, Member, Board of Governors
Federal Reserve System

Lewis S. Ranieri, Chairman and CEO
Ranieri and Co., Inc.

1   Securitization: A New Era in American Finance

Leon T. Kendall

Securitization is one of the most important and abiding innovations to emerge in financial markets since the 1930s. It is changing the face of American and world finance. A revolution has occurred in the way the borrowing needs of consumers and businesses are met. The historic use of financial intermediaries to gather deposits and lend them to those seeking funds is being supplemented and even replaced by securitization processes that bypass traditional intermediaries and link borrowers directly to money and capital markets. A complex array of loan originators, funders, securities conduits, credit enhancers, investment bankers, and domestic and global investors are displacing traditional portfolio lenders, local thrifts, and banks. Deregulation and the competition it fosters has atomized rather than concentrated finance in America. Today over two-thirds of all home loans are being securitized. Further, about one-seventh of outstanding auto loans and one-fourth of outstanding credit card receivables have been securitized. And the process continues to expand into new fields. In addition, a whole new family of synthetic securities, premised on securitized cash flows, has been created and sold to individual and institutional investors under names like CMOs (collateralized mortgage obligations), IOs (interest-only strips), POs (principal-only strips), PACs (planned amortization classes), TACs (targeted amortization classes), inverse floaters, and other so-called derivatives.

Securitization Defined

What is securitization? Why did it come on the scene now? How does it operate? Securitization can be defined as a process of packaging individual loans and other debt instruments, converting the package into a security or securities, and enhancing their credit status or rating to further their sale to third-party investors. The process converts illiquid individual loans or debt instruments which cannot be sold readily to third-party investors into liquid, marketable securities. These new debt instruments are often termed "asset-backed securities" because each pool is backed by specific collateral rather than by the general obligation of the issuing corporation or instrumentality. Investors purchase a proportionate share of the assets and the bundle of rights linked to the assets, not a general obligation typical of traditional corporate debt.

The asset-backed security is structured under applicable laws to stand on its own and pass through timely payment of interest and principal to investors. The issuer makes no commitment to provide cash to securityholders except for those funds flowing from the bundle of rights created from the enhanced collateral pool.

A second definition of securitization is attributable to John Reed, chairman of Citicorp. Before an audience at the Kellogg Graduate School of Management he stated, "Securitization is the substitution of more efficient public capital markets for less efficient, higher cost, financial intermediaries in the funding of debt instruments." This definition speaks to the way banks, thrifts, and other portfolio lenders and investors operated during the pre-deregulation, cartel era of 1933–1980 with very high costs and highly structured ways of doing business. So long as laws, regulations, and the lack of low-cost technology precluded free entry into the loan origination business, banks and other deposit-type institutions were sheltered from price competition. Potential competitors could not take advantage of the cost umbrella they erected. When new entrants and price competition were permitted, however, the high-cost portfolio lenders were at risk. Deregulation created fertile ground for a new family of financial products that would threaten traditional intermediaries. The market share of securitized products in residential home lending, auto lending, and credit card receivables grew rapidly, and securitized techniques expanded into more and more market sectors.

The experiences of the late 1970s and the 1980s suggest that the introduction of securitization into a financial market responds favorably to the following conditions: A severe shortage of funds in the sector due to a withdrawal of traditional lenders, a desire by investors for high yields on rated investments, and healthy spreads for Wall Street firms. A willingness on the part of regulators or legislators to change laws and regulations to accommodate securitization can accelerate the process. These conditions were operative in the United States during the 1980s. On the investor side the shift in the way Americans save, to pension funds and other managed accounts, placed pools of capital in the hands of investment managers who were willing and able to respond to the new funding techniques.

The Securitization Structure

The process involved in structuring an asset-backed security is depicted graphically below. Figure 1.1 sets forth the basic steps necessary to create a securitized issue. The process involves six key participants. The loan originator makes the loans and may service them as well. Servicing includes the collection of payments and the other steps necessary to assure that the borrower meets his or her obligations and that the rights of investors in the collateral are protected throughout the life of the contract.

The trust is a special purpose entity created solely to purchase the loans and issue asset-backed securities based on that collateral. It may be a subsidiary of the originator or of the investment bank that underwrites and distributes the securities. The trust structure is employed because under law it is exempt from taxes, permits the originator to

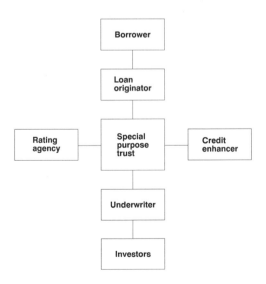

Figure 1.1
Basic structure of asset-backed securities

treat the transaction as a loan sale, and reduces liability for the originator and issuer. The trust also controls the collateral, administers the collection of cash flows, and passes through both interest and principal to the investors.

Since most securitized assets are sold with double-A or triple-A ratings from a national credit-rating agency, the rating agencies are involved in the securitization process. In the case of home mortgages issued by agencies backed by the full faith and credit of the U.S. government or the government-sponsored enterprises (GSEs), Fannie Mae or Freddie Mac, the market does not call for ratings. Ratings, however, are an important element for all securities not guaranteed by such agencies. One reason is because many regulated investors, such as life insurance companies and pension funds, are not allowed by regulation to purchase securities rated below investment grade. The market accepts ratings as a good proxy for the due-diligence investigation investors would have to conduct on individual securities and even individual loans serving as collateral. The market acceptance of ratings creates a family of tradable products and thereby furnishes investors with both an expectation of liquidity and a basis for market pricing.

The guarantee of highly rated credit enhancers or overcollateralization are enhancements added to the bundle of rights purchased by investors. This is done when the collateral or pooled loans will not provide sufficient protection for investors against credit losses in the worst of times. Rating agencies require additional credit enhancement to be certain the cash flows from the bundle of rights in the securitized issue are of sufficient quality to meet the promised payments of interest and principal in catastrophic circumstances. A bank letter of credit or a financial insurance company guarantee policy from a highly rated company is one method of enhancement. Overcollateralization, a senior subordinated debt structure, or a reserve account established to protect cash flows in the event of defaults on underlying loans are other techniques.

The originator or pool sponsor typically will negotiate with the rating agencies the type and size of the excess collateral or guaranty policy. The size of the enhancement is dictated by the credit rating desired. For the highest triple-A rating, the rating agencies are likely to insist that the level of protection be sufficient to shield cash flows against circumstances as severe as those experienced during the Great Depression of the 1930s. This requirement makes it highly desirable for issuers to have a body of historical data on the experience of their loans during good times and bad. Where it does not exist, the rating agencies will err on the side of conservatism and require larger enhancements.

The investment bank or underwriter is responsible for pricing and marketing the securities to investors. Since it has an ongoing relationship with institutional investors, it can provide ready counsel on what the market will buy and the price at which it will buy it. The personnel of investment banking firms are especially skilled at structuring the classes of securities to be issued by the trust and in setting the offering prices on the various classes of securities created. They also have substantial knowledge of the legal requirements that must be met in tailoring securities to fit the legal needs of regulated institutional purchasers.

Investors play a vital role in the success of securitized markets. In fact, without their willing participation, only a limited market would exist. The securities offered must meet their funding requirements, such as matching the potential insurance claims or retirement obligations they face. The desire they have for short-term or long-term debt, the degree to which they want fixed-rate or floating-rate interest payments, their managerial desire for yield to beat a nationally recognized portfolio measurement index, the need to meet new regulatory standards—all can affect their appetite for securitized assets and the form of such assets that they will buy.

Table 1.1 sets forth the value added through securitization by contrasting the investment attributes of individual loans and a pool of securities created from these loans.

Table 1.1
Value added through securitization

Loans	Securities
Illiquid	Liquid/tradable
Collateral valuation subjective and periodic	Market determines value—in some cases daily
Originator assesses risk	Third parties—rating agencies and enhancers—assess risk
Originators' operating costs high	Originators' operating costs low
Investor market local	Investor market national/global
Limited terms and rates offered borrowers	Buffet of terms and rates offered borrowers

Modern Origins of Securitization

The modern foundations of securitization can be traced to the residential mortgage market in the late 1970s. The strong desire for home ownership at a time when house prices were escalating over 6 percent a year and the primary funders of housing, the savings and loan associations, were being disintermediated created the primary condition necessary for securitization: a funding shortfall. The financial community, in the form of the Bank of America and Wall Street, responded. They were successful over time in changing tax laws to permit the tax-free pass-through of cash flows from home loans to mortgage securities, thereby avoiding double taxation, in modernizing the investment powers of institutional investors and in developing the computer technology needed to create new securities out of cash flows and to track the cash flows. The contributions of what today are called government-sponsored entities (GSEs), Freddie Mac and Fannie Mae, were material. They created uniform underwriting standards, monitored them, and offered investors quasi-government guarantees on securitized products at highly attractive yields. Investors learned to shift their focus from the credit quality of the underlying loans and the standing of the originator to the timing of cash flows and the potentials of prepayment risk.

Experience gained with mortgage-backed securities was extended to automobile financing under the acronym CARS and to credit card receivables under the banner CARDS. A list of the types of debt markets where securitization has supplied funds to borrowers during the 1980s and 1990s appears in table 1.2. The securitization process has also been exported to other economies around the world, albeit with modest success. This limited success is due to international differences in consumer borrowing patterns and debt levels, fundamental differences in the structure of financial institutions, and differences in legal and regulatory systems. Efforts to expand the reach of securitization continue both nationally and globally.

Basic Requirements for Securitization

Seven basic requirements emerge from an analysis of successful securitization programs. These requirements are listed in table 1.3. A standardized risk contract gives all participants in the process confidence that the collateral exists in a form that will enable the parties at interest

Table 1.2
Financial assets securitized during the 1980s and 1990s

• Fixed-rate mortgages	• Equipment leases
• Adjustable-rate mortgages	• Mobile home loans
• Second mortgages	• Marine loans
• Home equity revolving lines of credit	• Recreational vehicle loans
• Auto loans	• SBA loans
• Commercial real estate loans	• Third world debt
• Credit card receivables	• Junk bonds

Table 1.3
Basic requirements for securitization

- Standardized contracts
- Grading of risk via underwriting
- Database of historic statistics
- Standardization of applicable laws
- Standardization of servicer quality
- Reliable supply of quality credit enhancers
- Computers to handle complexity of analysis

to meet their contractual obligations, including repossession and fore-closure, in a well defined and legally enforceable manner. The evaluation and grading of risk by professional underwriters using established standards serves to verify that the collateral exists and provides the parties at interest with the due diligence as to the nature of the risk. A database of historic statistics enables parties at interest to subject the pool to a range of stress tests to determine how it would perform under differing conditions. The existence of these safeguards provide significant benefits to the originators, assemblers, enhancers, investment bankers, and investors, as well as to the rating agencies. Without standards, the determination of the size of financial guarantees or excess collateral needed to enhance ratings to optimal levels for salability in the market becomes very difficult, and the price of such coverage prohibitive. Securitization can make efficient use of insurance principles and the bifurcation of cash flows, provided a reliable body of data on past performance is available for analysis.

Because a securitized security issue is a legal contract and institutional purchasers tend to be highly regulated entities, investors must be highly confident as to how federal, state, and local laws will affect their rights. A recognition that their rights will be handled in a uniform manner across state lines is critical to liquidity and efficient pricing and trading. Standards specifying the quality of servicers who administer the loans on the borrower level and the contract under which they will operate are also critical to successful securitization. The bankruptcy of the servicer or the sale of servicing rights cannot expose the investors to loss. If they can, the rating agencies will withhold a top credit rating from the issues.

The credit enhancer, typically a third-party bank or financial guaranty insurance company, is another element critical to the transaction. Under the "weakest link" concept of credit analysis practiced by credit-rating agencies, the rating on the security issue can be no higher than the rating of the weakest link in the transaction, and that is often the quality of the credit-enhancing entity. Each enhancer is rated individually, and if its rating changes, so may the ratings of all of the issues it has guaranteed. At times, enhancers have withdrawn from securitized markets for legal, regulatory, or risk management reasons and will no longer underwrite certain risks. Such action can jeopardize the volume of securitization in a financial market.

Finally, without computers to model securitized structures, to track cash flows, and to oversee the many detailed elements in transactions on a daily and monthly basis, the volume of securitized transactions would be much smaller, and those which were done would be much simpler. The landmark Bank of America mortgage pass-through security of 1977, for example, consisted exclusively of 8.5% loans because the administrators had not yet figured out how to commingle loans with different note rates in a single pool.

The Creation of Synthetic Securities

Understanding of securitization can be enhanced by differentiating natural securities from synthetic securities. Natural securities may be defined as debt instruments based on the direct payment of interest and principal by the obligor—home owner, auto buyer, business corporation—to the investor. Synthetic securities, or derivatives, involve the recycling or bifurcation of the cash flows or credit risk from the natural securities to create multiple securities with revised bundles of

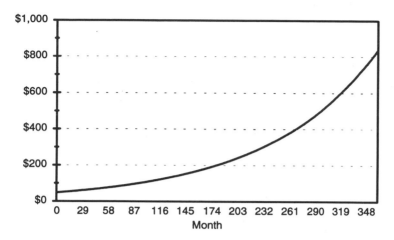

Figure 1.2
9.5%, thirty-year, $100,000 mortgage principal payments: No prepayment

rights and unique characteristics. Such structuring can expand the pool
of investors attracted to an investment market, increase the size of pool
offerings, and lower the aggregate cost to borrowers.

Billions of dollars worth of synthetic securities, or derivatives, have
been created from fixed-rate home mortgages. Take the standard, fully
amortized, fixed-rate home loan. If all borrowers in a securitized loan
pool paid back their obligations in accordance with the original schedule, the pass-through payments of principal would mirror the curve
in figure 1.2. However, American homeowners are highly unlikely to
stay in a home for thirty years, and even if they did, they are unlikely
to hold to the original loan repayment schedule. Experience has shown
that the typical household changes homes every seven years. There is
a predictable cyclicality and seasonality to both prepayments and
refinancing. If we take one thousand borrowers, the size and timing
of actual prepayments and repayments of loan principal can be estimated statistically.

The actual principal repayment curve will look more like that in
figure 1.3, a curve the market calls principal flows at a speed of 160
percent of the Public Securities Association (PSA) model.

Such natural cash flows can be recycled, bifurcated, and structured
into securities designed to take advantage of the shape of the Treasury
yield curve by assigning specific and prioritized cash flows to discrete
tranches. Figure 1.4 shows a four-tranche sequential Collateralized
Mortgage Obligation (CMO) structured out of the cash flows illus-

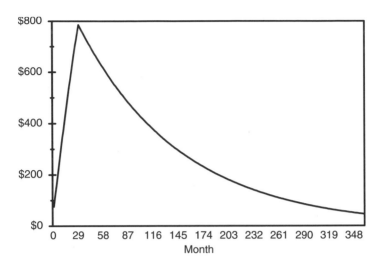

Figure 1.3
9.5%, thirty-year, $100,000 mortgage principal payments: 160% PSA

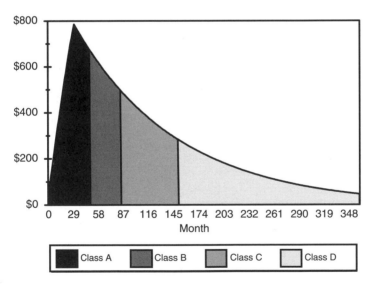

Figure 1.4
Four-class sequential CMO principal payments: 160% PSA

trated in figure 1.3. The first tranche receives all principal payments in the early years and is paid off in forty-eight months; the second tranche then begins to receive principal payments and is paid off in the eighty-fourth month, and so on. The effects of excessive repayments or a shortfall are absorbed differently by the various classes. Consequently, the market values of the longer tranches can be volatile. Investors seeking to minimize or to maximize interest rate risk have interesting choices.

The ability to bifurcate interest rate and credit risk and to reengineer risk profiles has led to the growth of a multibillion dollar mortgage-backed securities market. The front page of the prospectus of a REMIC (Real Estate Mortgage Investment Conduit) pool with over forty classes of separate securities created and offered to the market by Freddie Mac is shown in figure 1.5. Mortgage pass-through strips, in which the investment bankers and others strip out the interest component—interest-only strips (IO)—from the principal component, principal-only strips (PO), and sell each payment stream separately to different bond-class investors, have very special cash flow characteristics. Their values can react strongly to changes in interest rates and prepayment speeds. They are used widely in hedging transactions. The process has also moved well beyond home lending. There are active markets in synthetic securities based on auto loans, credit cards, home equity loans, boat loans and commercial property mortgages.

Public concerns regarding the volatility of derivatives and the losses suffered by corporations, municipalities, pension funds, and other institutional investors should be seen within the context of a long view. Financial markets learn quickly from mismanagement and abuse of new instruments and often are better for the experience.

Reasons for Success of Securitization

Securitization owes its success primarily to the fact that it has lowered the cost of moving funds from investors to borrowers. A market dominated by deposit-oriented financial intermediaries tends to internalize the various functions necessary to create and fund loans into individual institutions. Portfolio lenders become vertically integrated and as a group duplicate services. The specialization and division of labor are limited, and a quest for efficiencies is not a profit-maximizing technique. Securitization, by contrast, tends to increase the number of specialized participants competing at various stages of the lending and

Offering Circular Supplement
(To Offering Circular Dated August 1, 1993)

$1,502,630,670
Federal Home Loan Mortgage Corporation
Multiclass Mortgage Participation Certificates, Series 1671

The Federal Home Loan Mortgage Corporation ("Freddie Mac") is offering its Multiclass Mortgage Participation Certificates of the above Series (the "Multiclass PCs"). The Multiclass PCs will consist of the various "Classes" listed below. The Classes will receive principal and interest payments, in differing proportions and at differing times, from the cash flows provided by Freddie Mac "Gold PCs" and "Gold Giant PCs" with interest rates of 7% per annum (the "PCs"). Underlying the PCs are pools of fixed-rate, first lien, residential mortgages and mortgage participations (the "Mortgages"). See "General Information — Structure of Transaction" in this Supplement.

Freddie Mac guarantees to each "Holder" of a Multiclass PC (i) the timely payment of interest at the applicable "Class Coupon" and (ii) the payment of the principal amount of the Holder's Multiclass PC as described in this Supplement.

Freddie Mac will make interest and principal payments on each monthly "Payment Date," beginning March 15, 1994, on the Classes entitled to such payments. See "Payments" in this Supplement.

This Series will involve the creation of an "Upper-Tier REMIC Pool" and a "Lower-Tier REMIC Pool." Elections will be made to treat both REMIC Pools as "real estate mortgage investment conduits" ("REMICs") pursuant to the Internal Revenue Code. The R and RS Classes will be "Residual Classes" and the other Classes will be "Regular Classes." The Residual Classes will be subject to transfer restrictions. See "Certain Federal Income Tax Consequences" in this Supplement and in the Multiclass PC Offering Circular.

Investors should read this Supplement in conjunction with the documents listed at the bottom of page S-2.

The obligations of Freddie Mac under its guarantees of the Multiclass PCs are obligations of Freddie Mac only. The Multiclass PCs, including any interest thereon, are not guaranteed by the United States and do not constitute debts or obligations of the United States or any agency or instrumentality of the United States other than Freddie Mac. Income on the Multiclass PCs has no exemption under federal law from federal, state or local taxation. The Multiclass PCs are exempt from the registration requirements of the Securities Act of 1933 and are "exempted securities" within the meaning of the Securities Exchange Act of 1934.

Class	Original Principal or Other Amount(1)	Class Type(2)	Class Coupon	Interest Type(2)	CUSIP Number	Final Payment Date(3)	Weighted Average Life at 250% PSA(4)	Class	Original Principal or Other Amount(1)	Class Type(2)	Class Coupon	Interest Type(2)	CUSIP Number	Final Payment Date(3)	Weighted Average Life at 250% PSA(4)
A	$ 44,491,855	PAC I	4.75%	FIX	3133T35M6	April 15, 2005	1.1 Yrs	ME	$ 54,496,272	PAC III	(5)	FLT	3133T36L7	February 15, 2024	3.5 Yrs
B	55,451,957	PAC I	5.00	FIX	3133T35N4	May 15, 2011	2.5	MF	15,090,952	PAC III	(5)	INV	3133T36M5	February 15, 2024	3.5
C	38,108,556	PAC I	5.25	FIX	3133T35P9	January 15, 2014	3.5	N	60,662,974	TAC	(5)	FLT	3133T36N3	February 15, 2024	6.0
D	62,553,047	PAC I	5.75	FIX	3133T35Q7	November 15, 2016	4.5	NA	47,992,369	TAC/AD	(5)	FLT	3133T36P8	December 15, 2022	3.7
E	92,002,596	PAC I	5.95	FIX	3133T35R5	November 15, 2019	6.0	NB	14,509,491	TAC/AD	(5)	INV	3133T36Q6	December 15, 2022	3.7
F	103,208,470	PAC I	6.25	FIX	3133T35S3	March 15, 2022	8.0	O	13,576,951	TAC	(5)	INV	3133T36R4	February 15, 2024	6.0
G	80,750,141	PAC I	6.50	FIX	3133T35T1	August 15, 2023	11.0	P	8,088,397	TAC	(5)	INV	3133T36S2	February 15, 2024	6.0
HA	17,347,711	PAC I	(5)	FLT/DLY	3133T35U8	January 15, 2024	15.0	QA	74,164,110	CPT	(5)	FLT/DLY	3133T36T0	February 15, 2024	14.3
HB	7,067,586	PAC I	(5)	INV/DLY	3133T35V6	January 15, 2024	15.0	QB	16,580,976	CPT	(5)	INV/DLY	3133T36U7	February 15, 2024	14.3
I	12,942,835	PAC I	7.00	FIX	3133T35W4	February 15, 2024	20.0	QC	15,203,643	CPT	(5)	INV/DLY	3133T36V5	February 15, 2024	14.3
J	209,733,333	PAC I	(5)	FLT	3133T35X2	December 15, 2022	4.3	QD	2,056,206	SUP	(5)	FLT	3133T36W3	February 15, 2024	23.3
JA	30,000,000	PAC I	(5)	FLT	3133T35Y0	January 15, 2024	4.7	QE	587,488	SUP	(5)	INV	3133T36X1	February 15, 2024	23.3
JB	250,000,000	NTL(PAC I)	(5)	INV/IO	3133T35Z7	January 15, 2024	—	S	40,139,969	TAC/AD	(5)	FLT	3133T36Y9	February 15, 2024	5.4
JC	10,246,667	PAC I	(5)	FLT	3133T36A1	January 15, 2024	12.6	TA	50,000,000	CPT/SCH	(5)	FLT	3133T36Z6	February 15, 2024	4.6
KA	68,504,546	PAC II	(5)	FLT	3133T36B9	February 15, 2024	3.5	TB	50,000,000	NTL(SCH)	(5)	INV/IO	3133T37A0	February 15, 2024	—
KB	19,572,728	PAC II	(5)	INV	3133T36C7	February 15, 2024	3.5	U	53,519,959	TAC/AD	(5)	FLT	3133T37B8	February 15, 2024	5.4
KC	29,359,091	NTL(PAC II)	(5)	INV/IO	3133T36D5	February 15, 2024	—	V	26,757,840	TAC/AD	(5)	INV	3133T37C6	February 15, 2024	5.4
KT	69,499,060	NTL(PAC II/TAC)	(5)	INV/IO	3133T36E3	February 15, 2024	—	W	2,140	TAC/AD	(5)	INV/IO	3133T37D4	February 15, 2024	5.4
L	10,139,576	PAC II	7.00	FIX	3133T36F0	February 15, 2024	12.0	Z	25,000,000	SUP	7.00%	FIX/Z	3133T37E2	February 15, 2024	16.9
MA	57,182,896	PAC III	(5)	FLT	3133T36G8	February 15, 2024	3.5	ZA	7,000,000	TAC	6.91069	FIX/Z	3133T37F9	February 15, 2024	15.7
MB	16,337,971	PAC III	(5)	INV	3133T36H6	February 15, 2024	3.5	R	0	NPR	0	NPR	3133T37G7	February 15, 2024	—
MC	30,000,000	PAC III	(5)	FLT	3133T36J2	February 15, 2024	3.5	RS	0	NPR	0	NPR	3133T37H5	February 15, 2024	—
MD	11,538,462	PAC III	(5)	INV	3133T36K9	February 15, 2024	3.5								

(1) Subject to proportionate increase as described under "Increase in Size" in this Supplement. The amount shown for a Notional Class is its original notional principal amount and does not represent principal that will be paid; see "Payments — Interest" in this Supplement.
(2) See "Description of Multiclass PCs — Standard Definitions and Abbreviations for Classes" in the Multiclass PC Offering Circular. The type of Class with which the notional principal amount of a Notional Class will be reduced is indicated in parentheses.
(3) See "Final Payment Dates" in this Supplement.
(4) Determined as described under "Prepayment and Yield Analysis" in this Supplement, and subject to the assumptions and qualifications in that section. Prepayments will not occur at the assumed rate of 250% PSA or any other constant rate, the actual weighted average rates of any or all of the Classes are likely to differ from those shown, perhaps significantly.
(5) The Floating Rate and Inverse Floating Rate Classes will bear interest as described under "Terms Sheet — Class Coupons" in this Supplement.

The Multiclass PCs are offered by Kidder, Peabody & Co. Incorporated (the "Underwriter") from time to time in negotiated transactions at varying prices to be determined at the time of sale, plus accrued interest from February 1, 1994 on the Fixed Rate and Delay Classes and from February 15, 1994 on the Floating Rate and Inverse Floating Rate Classes other than the Delay Classes (the "Non-Delay Classes"). The Multiclass PCs are offered by the Underwriter when, as and if issued, subject to delivery by Freddie Mac and acceptance by the Underwriter, to prior sale and to withdrawal, cancellation or modification of the offer without notice. It is expected that the Regular Classes (other than the W Class, which will be available (in book-entry form) for deposit at any Federal Reserve Bank, and that delivery of the W Class and the Residual Classes (in certificated form) will be made at the offices of the Underwriter, New York, New York, on or about February 28, 1994 (the "Closing Date").

Kidder, Peabody & Co.
Incorporated

Offering Circular Supplement Dated January 4, 1994

Figure 1.5
The front page of a prospectus
Source: Freddie Mac.

funding process and encourages new entrants and price and product competition.

On the investor side, securitization's major contribution has been to convert nonrated, relatively illiquid loans into rated, highly liquid, tradable securities at attractive market prices. Furthermore, in some cases securitization facilitates the pricing of these securities on a daily basis. For some debt instruments, it provides a heretofore nonexistent secondary market for risk assets. Linking local debt markets to the national capital markets, it eliminates the regional pockets of monopoly power that marked bank and thrift markets for decades. Today, home loan interest rates and terms are essentially national, varying relatively little from one section of the country to another, or from big towns to small.

The benefits of the securitization process to the various participants in the lending process are set forth in table 1.4.

The national credit rating agencies and the private financial guarantors, along with Freddie Mac and Fannie Mae in the home loan field,

Table 1.4
Benefits of securitization

Benefits to consumers-borrowers
1. Lower cost of funds
2. Increased buffet of credit forms
3. Competitive rates and terms nationally and locally
4. Funds available consistently

Benefits to originators
1. Ability to sell assets readily
2. Profits on sales
3. Increased servicing income
4. More efficient use of capital

Benefits to investors
1. High yields on rated securities
2. Liquidity
3. Enhanced diversification
4. Potential trading profits

Benefits to Wall Street (investment bankers)
1. New product line
2. Continuous flow of originations and fees
3. Trading volume and profits
4. Potential for innovation and market expansion

have become the interpreters and protectors of the quality of credit in the securitized securities market. They are able to do this because they possess the most comprehensive information on the risk environment through which these bundles of rights must pass from origination to pay-off or maturity. The credit rating agencies welcomed the emergence of ratable securities as a new product line that would increase corporate revenues through new issues and subsequent rating review fees. The financial guarantee companies also viewed the field as a new source of potential business—and risk.

For one important class of participants securitization has been a mixed blessing. The portfolio lenders—the savings and loan associations and banks that formerly dominated residential and consumer lending and set prices locally and regionally—saw their profit margins under pressure and their market share of loan originations decline. The savings and loan market share of mortgage originations shrank from 38 percent in 1985 to 19 percent in 1994. Funding of home loans moved through the GSEs, Freddie Mac and Fannie Mae, at an increasing pace, with the GSEs accommodating the smallest originator on virtually the same terms as traditional originators. As the high-cost operators in the home loan and consumer lending markets, traditional lenders found themselves under pressure to meet national lending rates linked to the capital markets, and to do so on a daily basis.

The portfolio institutions suffered a loss of monopoly power in product offering and pricing, a loss of the information advantage they held formerly as local lenders, a loss of insulation from new market entrants, and a loss of traditional customers, particularly the larger ones. Short of a wide-ranging reregulation of banking and consumer finance and restrictions on competition, it is difficult to see how portfolio lending institutions can regain their former status.

Portfolio lenders themselves have become important producers of securitized product, both as originators and sellers of loans and as purchasers of securitized paper. Through such activity, desirable from the view of the individual entity, they were in a sense digging their own graves. Interestingly, in the United Kingdom securitization in the residential mortgage field, after a strong introductory surge, waned because the building societies, the U.K. version of portfolio thrifts and the primary home loan originators, determined not to originate or invest in securitized product. In fact, they competed aggressively against it through price and terms.

The Next Level of Securitization

The development of securitization in financial markets in the United States has passed through three stages. The first stage was the conversion of traditional portfolio debt instruments into pass-through securities. Interest and principal with appropriate enhancements are purchased by third party investors, and a secondary market develops. Risks of prepayment, interest rate changes, and residual credit exposure also pass through to the investor. The number of investors willing to buy the risk asset is limited by the nature of the original loan contracts and the nature of the security. A need to match the security with the funding requirements of investors becomes apparent.

Bifurcation of cash flows or credit risk into investor-friendly tranches marks the second stage of securitization. Establishing the predictability of cash flows and ordering them with serial priorities permits the creation of securities with terms closer to what investors, especially major institutional investors, seek. The restructuring of one home loan pool into three-year, five-year, and ten-year notes based on prepayment experience, as well as interest-only and principal-only tranches and even more exotic instruments increased the size and interest of the investor group and the efficiency of pricing. The synthetic securities or derivatives developed through this process have created both value and notoriety.

The third stage of securitization is likely to involve the recycling of securitized issues, recombining outstanding issues into new securities. The exercise will be investor driven and designed by investment bankers to provide investors with cash flows from seasoned pools of debt instruments in new forms that meet their funding needs. The commercial real estate property field is one area where such processes are underway. Private placements can be a logical outgrowth of these developments. Greater sophistication in reengineering cash flows and a quest for values in lesser quality tranches can be expected. As is the case in the larger, more public markets, the credit-rating agencies will play the vital role of custodian of credit quality in securitized markets.

The development of securitization was a market-driven process. It grew most vigorously in areas of need, where there was a shortfall in the supply of capital. So long as society encourages competition among financial institutions, securitization is likely to grow. A second building block has been the growing public access to information on borrowers, collateral, and other elements of risk. Such information, once the province of traditional portfolio lenders, is now widely available. Furthermore, the ability of credit-rating agencies to convert this knowledge into ratings viewed as reliable by the market accelerated trading and liquidity. The rating agencies, rather than the local portfolio lenders, have become the gatekeepers overseeing access to capital markets by borrowers. Market tests can be met by quality of collateral rather than by the credit standing of the originator/issuer.

Widespread access to information and the recognition that pools of loan contracts embodied predictable cash flows were major breakthroughs. When investment professionals recognized they could apply computer modeling and bifurcate, combine and recombine cash flows, and offer investors highly rated products tailored to their needs at attractive yields, a whole new family of investment products was created. The willingness of regulators and legislatures to accommodate the needs of securitized markets, and the conviction that the fresh air of competition would be good for consumers, business, and the economy had a salubrious effect.

Growth did not occur without problems and pitfalls. Although the securitized structures that rest on collateral-based lending have fared very well and credit losses have been minimal, the exposure of some derivative securities to rapidly changing interest rates has exposed some investors to market losses. Calls for regulation of securitization processes have reached Congress, but onerous prohibitions are unlikely. Fraud has visited the field and is likely to come again. The need for education and greater knowledge among investors, including sophisticated investors, of the special risks implicit in this new breed of securities is great. At times they seem to be behind the knowledge curve and face the risk of being oversold by investment bankers.

The authors of the subsequent chapters of this text, the leaders of securitization in a sense, were requested to include in their writings the most important lessons they learned about the problems and pitfalls implicit within the new field. If experience, indeed, is the best teacher, education from those who learned by firsthand experience may very well be second best, and decidedly less costly.

2 Securitization's Role in Housing Finance: The Special Contributions of the Government-Sponsored Enterprises

Leland C. Brendsel

Many assets have been securitized, but nowhere is the process more advanced than in the mortgage market. At no time was this more evident than in 1993, when a record trillion dollars of residential mortgage loans were made in one year, and 60 percent of those loans were securitized—packaged into mortgage-backed securities—primarily by Freddie Mac, Fannie Mae, and Ginnie Mae. The sharp increase in mortgage lending that occurred in 1993 would not have been possible without the mortgage-backed securities market, which provided the financing for the large volume of mortgage borrowers who rushed to reduce their mortgage payments by refinancing their mortgage loans. As refinancing subsided in 1994, securitization continued to finance housing for millions of American families. Table 2.1 compares the scope of the market for mortgage-backed securities to that of other securities markets.

One way to approach securitization is to understand how institutions use it to fund assets. The real story is the benefits that securitization brings to the housing finance system and to consumers.

Today's housing finance system provides the most reliable, low-cost source of funds to home buyers possible. To explain how, I will start with a simple example about what happens when an individual home buyer from Evanston, Illinois, gets a mortgage loan. A local lender might quote an interest rate of 9 percent in the current market for a thirty-year, fixed-rate loan.

Chances are, before quoting that rate, the lender will check the prices that Freddie Mac is posting to buy loans. The lender may also check the prices that our competitor, Fannie Mae, or some other institutions are quoting, but the example will focus on Freddie Mac. Checking our prices is easy because our computer system is linked directly to lenders' own systems. Lenders that sell to Freddie Mac receive on their

Table 2.1
Volume in securities markets: 1994
($ billions)

	Mortgage-backed securities	Municipal securities	Corporate bonds	Treasury securities
New issues	362	204	370	2,100
Outstanding	1,500	1,200	1,300	3,100
Estimated daily trading volume	45	3	15	192

Source: Public Securities Association.
Note: Mortgage-backed securities include only those issued by Freddie Mac, Fannie Mae, or Ginnie Mae.

own screens the current prices that we will pay for mortgage loans to be delivered to us according to a specified schedule. In fact, they can commit to sell us the loans by computer as well.

These lenders can be assured that they can sell a loan to us at our posted price as long as they make that mortgage loan according to our underwriting guidelines, which assist lenders in assessing whether a potential borrower will be able to make payments on time and whether the property is adequate collateral.

Knowing the price we will pay, the lender knows the rate it must charge the consumer to make and service the loan for a profit. Once we purchase this loan, we package it along with many similar mortgages into pools and create mortgage-backed securities. We call our securities Mortgage Participation Certificates or PCs. Generically, they are called conventional mortgage-backed securities or pass-through securities. We guarantee the investors in these securities that they will get paid even if the borrowers default on the mortgages.

This process of securitization—that is, pooling the loans and using them to back guaranteed mortgage-backed securities—turns individual mortgages into homogeneous, liquid instruments that can be traded efficiently in capital markets.

Freddie Mac commits to purchase loans from lenders and sells securities every business day. We distribute these securities through Wall Street dealers, which in turn distribute them to investors. The investors could be banks, thrifts, or pension funds. They could be worldwide investors as well. The price we receive for these securities determines the price we pay lenders for the mortgages, including an increment for our costs of operation and a return to our shareholders.

This example illustrates how we buy loans for cash, which is one of two ways we purchase mortgages and create mortgage-backed securities. The other method is a "swap" transaction, in which we exchange securities for a pool of mortgages sold to Freddie Mac by a lender, and the lender then may sell the securities.

The result under either method is that the borrower in Evanston gets the mortgage, and the mortgage interest rate is determined by the yield required by the marginal investor, whether it is a California pension fund or a bank in Chicago or Japan. Securitization enables the individual home buyer to compete for credit in worldwide capital markets, and it gives American families the most consistently competitive mortgage rates possible. This simple story reflects a quarter century of development of mortgage securitization.

Freddie Mac was chartered by Congress in 1970 to create a secondary mortgage market for conventional loans. We have been instrumental in the development of this market ever since. An example will show how far the market has evolved. In 1981, the year I joined the company, Freddie Mac purchased only one type of loan, once a week. Now we buy every major mortgage product, whether it is thirty-year, twenty-year, or fifteen-year fixed-rate mortgages, or various kinds of adjustable-rate mortgages. We buy these loans continuously, and we change prices continuously—on average about five times an hour—in response to changes in the capital markets. Because lenders are now linked into the capital markets, they tend to change the rates they quote consumers far more frequently.

Origins of the Secondary Mortgage Market

At the time Freddie Mac was chartered, there was a growing secondary market for government loans, that is, loans insured by the Federal Housing Administration (FHA) or guaranteed by the Department of Veterans Affairs (VA). This secondary market was provided by Fannie Mae, which bought those loans for its portfolio, and by Ginnie Mae, which was beginning to securitize government-backed loans.

Conventional mortgages, the bulk of the market, did not have a well-developed secondary market. These loans were primarily originated and held by thrifts, making the cost and availability of conventional mortgage credit unpredictable. For example, when interest rates rose above the levels thrifts could pay for deposits, thrifts lost their source of funds for mortgages. Plus, growing areas of the country with high demand for mortgages tended to have a relatively low supply of deposits.

Thrifts occasionally sold mortgage loans to one another in a very elementary form of a secondary market. If whole loan trading were more efficient, it could have addressed regional imbalances in mortgage and deposit flows. The trading of whole loans was cumbersome, however. For every loan package, the purchaser was confronted with performing a lot of due diligence, examining loan documents that varied from state to state—or institution to institution. Freddie Mac was created to address the problems associated with trading whole loans in the secondary market.

In the 1970s Freddie Mac laid the foundation for a successful conventional secondary market and the securitization of those mortgages. We did the same types of things that are done today to securitize other types of assets: standardizing underwriting and appraisal practices; developing uniform instruments to be used by lenders nationwide; and designing the security.

These tasks had been largely accomplished by the beginning of the 1980s, but the conventional mortgage-backed securities market was still quite small. Freddie Mac's mortgage purchases in 1981, for example, were under $4 billion, and we had just $20 billion dollars in securities outstanding. The conventional mortgage-backed securities business took off in the 1980s, however, spurred by a more favorable accounting and regulatory environment, growing investor confidence, and the demand created by a faltering thrift industry.

Freddie Mac Today

Freddie Mac began as a small, government-controlled company to facilitate trading among thrifts. We evolved with the market, and by 1990 we had become a publicly held, stockholder-owned company listed on the New York Stock Exchange. Our current market capitalization of about $10 billion puts us about eightieth on the Standard and Poor's 500.

Even though Freddie Mac is privately owned, we, like Fannie Mae, are a corporation chartered by the United States government. We are one of only about ten institutions with that status. Being a government-sponsored enterprise (GSE) was important to establishing a nationwide secondary market and securitizing mortgages. GSE status enabled us to gain more rapid investor acceptance and to avoid many of the regulatory impediments that other issuers would have faced.

Though we are often mistaken for a government agency, Freddie Mac is a private company for which the government has never appropriated any money. In fact, we are among the nation's largest corporate federal taxpayers. Our profitable operations have enabled us to build our capital base, through both retained earnings and issues of stock.

In our capital planning, we subject the company to a stress test; that is, we determine whether we have enough capital to survive ten years of extremely adverse conditions. The Office of Federal Housing Enterprise Oversight (OFHEO) is currently developing its own stress test that will be used to set a risk-based capital standard for Freddie Mac and Fannie Mae. Such a dynamic, forward-looking capital standard is unprecedented in financial markets. In the meantime, Freddie Mac has been classified "adequately capitalized" by OFHEO, the highest possible rating.

Today Freddie Mac is a wholesale financial institution. We buy mortgages from about two thousand mortgage lenders across the country, and we finance these mortgages through a worldwide network of securities dealers. In 1994, in contrast to the $4 billion that we purchased in 1981, we purchased $124 billion of mortgages and securitized just under that amount. That is one loan purchased every five seconds of every business day. These mortgages financed homes for 1.3 million families. Currently there are almost one-half trillion dollars in Freddie Mac mortgage-backed securities outstanding, compared to $20 billion in 1981. Unquestionably, we must have a highly efficient operation.

Our operations include purchasing and pooling mortgages, and creating and guaranteeing securities. We have a small broker/dealer that, along with the Wall Street houses, makes markets and distributes our securities. Our operations also include collecting payments from lenders and making payments to investors. These operations are located in our McLean, Virginia, headquarters and our five regional offices. About three thousand employees handle all these operations. Freddie Mac is, therefore, highly leveraged in terms of the amount of revenue per person, which carries with it requirements for highly trained people.

We have a large number of professionals who must be outstanding at operating large-scale information-processing and payments-processing systems. Managing credit risks is another basic skill we must have because we take the risk of loss on all the mortgages that we purchase. We must be skilled at financial management because we manage a large portfolio of mortgages that we do not sell. Finally, we must be outstanding at guarding the integrity of our securities. If investors do not have utmost confidence in the quality of the securities we issue, they will start to discount our securities in terms of price, and we will become uncompetitive relative to alternatives.

Three Keys to Securitization's Success

Securitization has given us an extraordinary system of financing housing in America. At the heart of this system are three key elements. First, securitization attracts private capital to housing through its ability to respond to investor needs. Second, securitization unleashes competitive forces that provide consumers lower cost credit and greater choice. Third, securitization brings greater stability to the housing finance system by managing the risks inherent in mortgage lending and investing.

In terms of securitization's ability to expand housing's investor base, consider the first conventional mortgage-backed securities. These were single-class securities that passed through the payments of the pool of mortgages to investors on a pro-rata basis. Securitization brought greater liquidity and predictability because the investors owned a share of a larger pool of similar mortgages, and Freddie Mac guaranteed the payment of principal and interest. Still, the range of investors was not very broad. In the early 1980s, the major investors in Freddie Mac's mortgage-backed securities were thrift institutions, which were also the major investors in whole mortgage loans.

Freddie Mac participated in a tremendous effort to find new ways of securitizing mortgages that would make them attractive to more investors. In 1983, Freddie Mac introduced the first multiclass mortgage-backed security—the Collateralized Mortgage Obligation (CMO). The unique thing about CMOs was that the investors in a pool of mortgages did not all receive the same pro-rata share of cash flows. Rather, cash flows from the pool of mortgages were allocated to investors based on a set of rules, enabling us to target investors whose portfolio needs were more suited to a particular profile of cash flows. Our first CMO had three classes—one that paid off very quickly, an intermediate class, and a longer term class—the total of which accounted for all the cash flows from the mortgages. About 40 percent of the first CMO was purchased by pension funds and insurance companies—the types of investors this innovation was designed to attract. CMOs brought an infusion of new capital to housing finance.

Much of the growth and evolution of financial markets has been affected by regulation and taxation, and the mortgage-backed securities market is no exception. In the early years there were limits to what multiclass mortgage securities could accomplish as issuers faced complex tax, accounting, and regulatory obstacles. The tax obstacles were addressed in the Tax Reform Act of 1986, which created Real Estate Mortgage Investment Conduits (REMICs)—multiclass mortgage securities like CMOs, but without the tax impediments. Since 1986, investors have seen tremendous growth and innovation in multiclass mortgage-backed securities.

The flexibility in structuring REMICs has made it possible to attract a wide variety of investors. A typical REMIC today contains ten to twenty different classes tailored to meet investors' portfolio needs, and past REMICs have had fifty or more classes. REMICs have reduced Freddie Mac's funding costs and have enabled us to decouple borrower and investor needs.

With the single-class, passthrough security, the design of the security must match the design of the mortgage. Introducing a new type of mortgage product requires creating a security that looks just like it. This is not the case with multiclass mortgage securities. As an example, many international investors prefer floating-rate securities tied to LIBOR, the London Inter-Bank Offer Rate. If consumers do not want LIBOR-indexed mortgages, then using REMICs, we can still meet the demand for LIBOR-indexed securities. A REMIC can resecuritize fixed-rate mortgages so that one class of investors receives an adjustable-rate security indexed to LIBOR and another class receives what is called an inverse floater, also tied to LIBOR but with cash flows that move in the opposite direction.

The expansion of the investor base for mortgage-backed securities fostered by REMIC structures helped minimize the impact of the shrinking investments in mortgages by thrift institutions in the late 1980s. Within ten years of the first issue, multiclass mortgage securities dominated conventional market financing. In 1993, about three-quarters of new Freddie Mac PCs were resecuritized as REMICs.

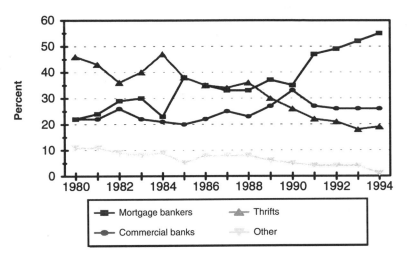

Figure 2.1
Lender share of conventional single-family originations
Source: Department of Housing and Urban Development; 1994 data through third quarter.

REMIC volume slowed considerably in 1994, however, with reduced origination volume and investor demand. Investors also chose simpler REMIC structures. In May 1994 Ginnie Mae issued its first REMIC, and the REMIC market continues to evolve.

The second point about securitization is that it unleashes competitive forces with the unbundling of the mortgage process. At one time a single institution, often a thrift, handled all aspects of mortgage lending—originating, servicing, credit risk taking, and investing. Now these four functions are frequently unbundled, with different companies specializing in the performance of each one, much like the rest of the financial system. Now that you do not have to fund a mortgage to be able to originate it, we are seeing a large increase in the number of mortgage lenders in the marketplace focused strictly on making mortgage loans. Figure 2.1 shows that as thrifts' share of originations declined, mortgage bankers' share increased.

Although it is a stretch to suggest that anyone with a modem and a fax machine can be a lender today, relatively little capital is required to start a mortgage banking operation in the 1990s, and even less to become a mortgage broker. Lenders lacking the necessary net worth can still originate loans for lenders qualified to sell into the secondary market. From a consumer standpoint, this easy entry fosters competition in service and in mortgage rates and products. Lenders are taking applications over the phone and making house calls. Although that may have been true of some small-town doctors in years past, it was unheard of in mortgage lending.

Competition in other parts of the business helps consumers too. In the servicing business, that is, collecting loan payments from borrowers and passing them through to Freddie Mac, competition has led to a smaller number of servicers. They are exploiting the economies of scale achieved with large servicing operations. Mortgage servicing is now traded actively and purchased by large, low-cost servicers competing to acquire this asset, which drives down mortgage rates further.

The third point about securitization is that it has brought greater stability to the housing finance system. The history of housing finance in the United States has been punctuated with a series of cataclysmic failures brought by excessive exposure to interest-rate and credit risks. Rising interest rates at the end of 1970s put the short-funded mortgage portfolios of the thrift industry and Fannie Mae under water. In the 1980s, loan defaults brought widespread failures in the mortgage insurance industry and excessive credit losses to FHA programs.

Securitization of mortgages helps reduce this type of exposure. One way is by effectively disbursing interest-rate risk. The interest-rate risk of mortgages is borne by thousands of investors who are managing it in their portfolios, rather than leaving this risk concentrated in a few institutions or one industry, as it was for decades in the thrift industry.

Credit risk is now being borne primarily by institutions like Freddie Mac, Fannie Mae, and mortgage insurers that are able to diversify this risk across the nation, rather than being isolated in local markets. Our analysis finds that the credit risk of a well-diversified, nationwide portfolio of loans is less than one-third the risk of a portfolio from a single region of the country. It is clearly much less than the risk of a portfolio of loans from a single city.

By managing risk well, by unleashing competitive market forces, and by attracting more investors, securitization provides Americans a reliable, low-cost source of financing for housing. Securitization has meant that while other sectors faced credit shortages, particularly in the latter part of the 1980s and the early 1990s, there has been no credit crunch in the residential mortgage market. Confidence that financing will be available spawns innovations because lenders can structure their businesses based on our being a reliable outlet for their loans.

In short, securitization and the global supply of capital it brings have revolutionized housing finance and given us a system that is the envy of the world. What will the future bring?

Challenges Ahead

We see several challenges in managing the credit risk on mortgages for the rest of the decade. One challenge comes from being in an economy in which inflation is relatively low. One of the most important factors determining the frequency of default on mortgage loans as well as the size of the losses is the amount of equity that borrowers have in their homes. With low rates of house-price appreciation, that equity builds very slowly, and more mortgages default. We must factor that into our underwriting and pricing. Default risk is more significant than in the past; no longer does rapid appreciation bail out bad credit decisions.

A second challenge in regard to managing credit risks is the pressure on the housing finance system to extend credit on unwise terms. This does not apply only to housing credit; it is also the case for commercial credit, particularly small business loans. These pressures arise from a variety of sources.

The mortgage market, for example, faced a great contraction as mortgage rates rose from 7 to 9 percent for thirty-year, fixed-rate loans in 1994. Originations fell by half from the beginning to the end of the year. Having built capacity for much higher volume, lenders increasingly competed to make loans, in part by approving more marginal borrowers.

At the same time, the lending industry is undertaking efforts to expand access to mortgage money, providing more credit to low-income and minority areas that may have been underserved. The industry is accepting the challenge of making credit available to more qualified borrowers in a way that promotes good lending and strong communities.

Maintaining incentives for quality lending in a fragmented industry presents another challenge in managing credit. When one institution both originated and held a loan in its portfolio, incentives for quality lending were clear. With today's increasing share of mortgage lending by mortgage bankers or brokers, which originate the loans and sell the risk into the secondary market, lenders have less of a stake in the performance of the loans over time. Lenders are the market's front line in maintaining credit quality. If traditional incentives to maintain quality cannot be relied upon, new ones have to be introduced. This is a classic principal/agent problem.

Securitization's future also includes a larger role in financing multifamily housing. The multifamily mortgage market is less than one-tenth the size of the single-family market—there are more than three trillion dollars in single-family mortgages outstanding and less than $300 billion in apartment loans. Just 12 percent of multifamily loans have been securitized, compared to about one-half of single-family loans (see table 2.2).

Although there is considerable room for increased multifamily securitization, I do not believe that securitization will ever become the dominant source of financing for multifamily housing, as it has for single-family housing, for several reasons. Multifamily loans are more like business loans than housing loans; evaluating them requires far more individual judgment and local market knowledge, and far more direct involvement by the lender—not only in making the loan, but in monitoring that loan over time. Multifamily properties are also much more difficult to appraise, and the transactions are much less likely to be standardized. When Freddie Mac buys multifamily loans, we re-underwrite every one; when we buy single-family loans we re-underwrite less than 5 out of every 100, relying on our customers to follow our guidelines. Replicating the work of the lender reduces the efficiency of secondary market financing for multifamily housing, but I do expect continued progress in the securitization of multifamily mortgages. In December 1994 Freddie Mac issued a $108 million REMIC backed by ten-year multifamily mortgages.

Securitization's future will also be driven by technological innovation, as it has been for the past decade. For example, the same information about a mortgage applicant will no longer have to be entered in multiple stages of the lending process. Links between lenders, appraisers, real estate brokers, mortgage insurers, title insurers, and secondary market institutions will be automated. These connections are beginning to be built. Freddie Mac is developing an electronic mortgage information network that will offer one-stop shopping for all these services in 1995.

This network will also carry the automated underwriting service that Freddie Mac is introducing in 1995 to more and more lenders. In developing this service, we did not just automate existing lending processes. We worked with lenders to redesign how mortgages are originated. This service will streamline mortgage originations, reduce costs, and improve lending decisions. Lenders will be able to approve a loan in minutes and close it in days, compared to the six or more weeks closing a loan can take today. Eventually, securitization will be immediate. As technological advances drive costs down, lenders may

Table 2.2
Securitized mortgage debt outstanding
($ billions)

	1980			Third quarter 1994		
	Total mortgage debt outstanding	Amount securitized	Percent securitized	Total mortgage debt outstanding	Amount securitized	Percent securitized
1–4 family						
Conventional	769	30	4	2773	1154	42
FHA/VA	196	95	48	503	444	88
Total	965	125	13	3276	1598	49
Multifamily						
Conventional	112	6	5	230	26	11
FHA	30	2	7	61	9	15
Total	142	8	6	291	35	12

Source: Freddie Mac, Fannie Mae, Federal Reserve Board, Department of Housing and Urban Development, Department of Veterans Affairs.

find their business even more competitive, while consumers will find faster service, lower costs, and greater home ownership opportunities.

Technology will create a wealth of information about the mortgage loans that back securities. To the extent investors value this information, the value will be reflected in the price they are willing to pay for the securities, again benefiting borrowers.

Investors' increasingly sophisticated computers and analytical tools will make it possible to evaluate all this information. When we first introduced conventional mortgage-backed securities in the 1970s, mortgages were pooled on the basis of a few characteristics—the maturity of the mortgage, the type of mortgage, and the rate on the mortgage. Less was more: viewing one PC as if it were the same as the next helped make the securities liquid. Over time, investors started to value more information so that they could predict how fast the mortgages in a particular pool were going to prepay. Freddie Mac has been on the cutting edge of providing comprehensive information to investors through the broker/dealer community, for example, updating mortgage pool characteristics over time. With advances in technology, not only can Freddie Mac disclose more, but investors can absorb the information. It is possible that we could go full cycle—giving investors all the information they would require to purchase individual whole loans.

Finally, I expect to see continued growth in securitization of residential mortgages during the remainder of the decade, though at a more moderate pace than the recent one. Over the past seven years, the average annual rate of growth in mortgage-backed securities outstanding was about 15 percent. In the next seven years, this growth will certainly moderate. Already, nearly one-half of outstanding conventional single-family mortgages have been securitized. Although this share will likely rise, perhaps to 60 percent, it will not get to 100 percent. Lending institutions will continue to hold mortgages in unsecuritized form in their portfolios. In 1994, for example, rising interest rates increased the popularity of adjustable-rate mortgages, which are less standardized and less likely to be sold into the secondary market.

Securitization has given us a strong system for financing housing. It will continue to evolve and offer the reliable mortgage capital that the nation's home buyers and lenders have come to expect. I am very proud of Freddie Mac's role in developing and improving this system, and I am confident in the future.

3　The Origins of Securitization, Sources of Its Growth, and Its Future Potential

Lewis S. Ranieri

The term *securitization* has an interesting origin. It first appeared in a "Heard on the Street" column of the *Wall Street Journal* in 1977. Ann Monroe, the reporter responsible for writing the column, called me to discuss the underwriting by Salomon Brothers of the first conventional mortgage pass-through security, the landmark Bank of America issue. She asked what I called the process and, for want of a better term, I said securitization. *Wall Street Journal* editors are sticklers for good English, and when the reporter's column reached her editor, he said there was no such word as securitization. He complained that Ms. Monroe was using improper English and needed to find a better term. Late one night, I received another call from Ann Monroe asking for a real word. I said, "But I don't know any other word to describe what we are doing. You'll have to use it." The *Wall Street Journal* did so in protest, noting that securitization was a term concocted by Wall Street and was not a real word. So, we have come a long way. A decade and a half ago securitization was not even a real word, and today we hold seminars on the concept.

The history of securitization goes back to the 1970s. At that time, housing in this country was funded by the thrift industry as portfolio lenders. The thrifts borrowed money from depositors and put loans on their books at fixed rates. In the mid to late 1970s, people started to worry about whether the existing home finance system, the thrift system, would be able to fund the growing demand for housing in the late 1970s and early 1980s. The demographics were powerfully positive. In other words, the baby boomers were reaching home-buying ages. Housing economists were forecasting a tremendous demand for funds for shelter because of the rise in family formations.

Thrifts were not in trouble in those days. The issue was simply whether the thrift balance sheets could grow fast enough to fund the nation's housing needs. There was a growing concern that people were going to wake up one day and find out that there was no mortgage money available. It was not an issue of the cost of funds. It was an issue of the availability of funds. The demographic forces were going to create a demand for funds greater than the ability of the thrifts to attract capital and grow their balance sheets.

Wall Street attempted to address the impending demand by coming up with an alternative source of funds. The idea was to create an adjunct to the thrift industry, not a replacement for it. The thrifts were viewed as central to the mortgage industry. Wall Street's contribution would be at the margin. The first attempt to expand the supply of funds for housing involved the use of mortgages as collateral. By using their home loans as collateral for long-term bonds, thrifts could get more funds for their lending operations and housing. These securities, called mortgage-backed bonds, were widely used by thrifts. Although mortgage-backed bonds provided thrifts with an inexpensive source of funds, they were highly inefficient. The early issues were overcollateralized by home loans at two or three times the face value of the bond issue. This inefficient use of collateral limited the ability of mortgage-backed bonds to solve the problem of limited funds available for mortgage lending.

There had to be a better way. Beginning in 1975, my mentor at Salomon Brothers, Bob Dall, worked with Lee Prussia and Woody Teal, senior officers of the Bank of America, for the better part of three years creating a security backed by home mortgages that was more efficient than the overcollateralized mortgage-backed bonds. They developed what we now know as pass-through techniques. The process involved legal, accounting, regulatory, tax, and a host of other issues. The first major challenge was finding an efficient tax vehicle for the new securities. Since there was no such thing as a mortgage security, there was no tax mechanism to convey the mortgages and the accompanying bundle of rights to the investor without creating double taxation and phantom income problems. This set of challenges was solved originally by attorney John Quisenberry, of Brown and Wood. He focused us on the provisions of the Federal Tax Code known as the grantor trust rules. These provisions, which were generally applied in connection with the taxation of trusts created to transfer assets from parents to children, were implemented to achieve a pass-through of the tax attributes of the mortgages to the investor.

In general, the Treasury did not object to what we were doing. The fact that our efforts would help provide housing was on our side.

However, the Treasury imposed certain limitations. It required that the grantor trusts be totally passive. This precluded any form of active management, bifurcation, or recombination of assets. Despite these limitations, in 1977 Bank of America issued through Salomon Brothers the first triple-A rated, conventional, mortgage-backed pass-through security.

Unfortunately, the victory of creating the first pass-through mortgage-backed security was followed by the total failure of the issue. We found, to our great horror, that these triple-A public securities were a legal investment in only about fifteen of the fifty American states at that time. The blue-sky laws, the state legal investment laws, offered no standing for a security of this type. Additionally, many investors had self-imposed prohibitions on investing in these securities. For example, when we studied the by-laws of the New York State Retirement System, a potentially large investor, we found a requirement that all mortgages be at least $1 million in size to qualify as an investment. This obviously was a reference to commercial mortgages, not single-family mortgages. However, this was the only reference to mortgages in the by-laws. Therefore, the lawyers determined that our triple-A securities did not qualify as a legal investment because the individual loans were not $1 million each. We had a wonderful concept that was a marketplace failure!

The years between 1977 and 1980 were extremely frustrating. During this period, the thrift industry and housing finance were exposed to a new problem. When free-market interest rates rose, the thrifts' regulated savings rates were exposed, and deposits left thrift offices. Additionally, as the yield curve inverted, the mismatch of maturities that resulted from borrowing short and lending long further eroded their net worth. The concern about the ability of thrifts to fund housing in the mid-1970s had escalated by the end of the decade as the thrifts appeared to be approaching the crisis stage.

As disintermediation escalated at the thrifts, their need for alternative sources of funding increased. They looked to the federal agencies for assistance. Until this time, it was politically unacceptable for the federal agencies to get involved in financing loans on the books of thrifts. Their mission was to support new housing and new home buyers, not to facilitate portfolio transactions. However, the problems of the thrift industry—that is, the disintermediation of funds, the illiquidity of their loan portfolios, and mounting losses—necessitated a change in direction among the federal agencies. They needed to assist the thrifts in converting their illiquid home loans into agency securities, thereby liquefying the loans and providing access to the repo markets of Wall Street.

At that time, there were three federal agencies that participated in the mortgage market, Fannie Mae, Ginnie Mae, and Freddie Mac. Fannie Mae was essentially the biggest savings and loan in America. It issued its own notes and bonds and used the funds to buy and hold mortgages on its balance sheet. Ginnie Mae, as we know it today, barely existed. Neither Fannie Mae nor Ginnie Mae were willing to participate in our efforts to fill the funds availability void. It was Freddie Mac that worked with us to overcome the roadblocks to securitization. At that time Freddie Mac, which was led by its president, Phil Brinkerhoff, was small and not a major force in the market place; but its powers as a federal agency proved to be the solution to our state legal and regulatory problems. As a federal agency, it was exempt from the state blue-sky laws and legal investment statutes. Because of these exemptions, Freddie Mac had the ability to issue mortgage pass-through securities, and Wall Street was then able to widely distribute the securities. The first securitization was consummated by Freddie Mac and Salomon Brothers from the mortgage portfolio of Perpetual Savings, a thrift headquartered in Washington, D.C. Securitization lessened the burden on thrifts and made Freddie Mac a major player. In turn, Freddie Mac gave us the preemption from state statutes and a conventional loan product we could sell to public investors nationally.

With disintermediation continuing, billions of dollars of old loans at thrifts were converted into securities. Fannie Mae, watching the business go by, decided to get into the act. As a result, the mortgage pass-through market went from nothing outstanding to billions outstanding almost overnight. This did not result from the issuance of new Freddie Mac and Fannie Mae securities based on new loans for housing but from securitizing a large portion of the mortgage loans in the portfolios of thrifts. Salomon Brothers and other Wall Street firms would find the customers, sell the deals, and pass them through the federal agencies.

Despite the involvement of the federal agencies and the use of their exemptions, there were still some problems in the market for mortgage-backed securities. One problem was that we could issue only thirty-year securities. In the capital markets, there are a limited number of investors with thirty-year money. There are fewer investors looking for thirty-year securities than for ten-year or two-year securities. In addition, as the thrifts continued to disintermediate, more and more of the burden of supporting housing was shifted from portfolio lenders to securitization and the capital markets. In an incredibly short period of time, the vehicle that was created to be an adjunct to the thrift system had become the substitute vehicle for the function that thrifts had historically performed in the economy. As securitization became the primary vehicle funding mortgage lending, the system began to break down again. With only thirty-year paper based on thirty-year loans to sell, we were forced to focus solely on thirty-year investors. We needed to broaden the investment appeal of the securitization market.

Additional problems occurred when Wall Street firms began trading mortgage-backed securities. The securities had a final maturity of up to thirty years but consisted of underlying assets that could prepay or default at any time. Because there was no accepted methodology to determine duration, it was very difficult to price the securities. It became imperative for a treaty or Wall Street convention to be developed that could be used by everyone to convert price to yield. The new technique was the fabled Ginnie Mae Formula, which is still in use today. Its methodology was simple. It assumed that no loan prepays for the first twelve years, and that on the first day of the thirteenth year, every loan prepays. Everyone understood that the yield produced by this formula could be the real investment yield only by accident. (And, I would hate to know what the odds are of that accident occurring!) This formula, which was used for the better part of the decade, was never intended to reflect true investment return. It was simply a convention that enabled Lehman Brothers, Salomon Brothers, Merrill Lynch, and others to compute prices and yields on a consistent basis. It simply enabled traders to talk to each other.

The next phase in the evolution of the securitization industry required a technique to predict accurately the average life of a pool of home mortgages. In order to expand this market and increase investor confidence, we needed to invest in some fundamental research into the nature of home loans and the ways mortgagees reacted to various economic conditions. One breakthrough occurred in a doctoral thesis by Helen Peters at the University of Pennsylvania (1979). She reported the real average life of mortgages and mortgage securities with some reliability. In addition to Peters's academic research, several Wall Street analysts, including Michael Waldman of Salomon Brothers and Dexter Senft of First Boston, made significant contributions.

It was difficult to sell mortgage securities in the early days of the mortgage securitization market due to its complexities and the lack of investor knowledge. It was necessary to convince investors that our mortgage-backed securities represented significantly better relative value than other securities in their portfolios. For example, I remember calling on Andy Carter, one of the great money managers of that day. In those days, single-A utility bonds were considered to be of very low credit quality because virtually all utilities had double-A or triple-A ratings. Therefore, a single-A utility then was comparable to a junk bond today. "Andy," I said, "if I can swap you out of a single-A utility into a full-faith-and-credit, guaranteed timely payment government bond, would you do it?" He replied, "Hey, stupid, of course I would." I then took out my Ginnie Mae certificate. In effect, I was offering him a Treasury bond even yield with a junk bond. That is literally how we sold mortgage securities even yield with single-A utilities.

The securitized mortgage product was not an easy concept to market; but by making the yield so cheap, we made it so that an investor could not help but pay attention. This overcame the complexities that we could not surmount or even at times explain. We were not able to convey to customers the average life of securities because none of us really knew how to compute it accurately. We created problems for the accountants because the pass-throughs were monthly pay securities and all other bonds were semiannual. In fact, after John Hancock bought a mortgage security, my customer came back two months later and said, "Gee, Lewis, I love this stuff but I can't buy any more because my back office is threatening to quit." We needed to overcome the bookkeeping inconvenience of a security that paid interest monthly.

The next innovation in securitization was the creation of the collateralized mortgage obligation, now universally called the CMO. Everyone on Wall Street and some in Washington took credit for the idea. In fact, however, the municipal bond industry had been using the concept of security tranches for decades in issues called serial bonds. In effect, we spent the better part of five years reinventing the wheel. If only we had consulted with municipal finance people, we would have been pointed in the right direction years earlier.

The CMO concept is very simple. Rather than look at a mortgage pool as a single group of thirty-year mortgages, the CMO concept approaches it as a series of unique annual cash flows each year for the next thirty years. It recognizes that cash flows are higher in the early years of the pool, and they can be carved up into separate tranches with a whole range of maturities from one to thirty years. Each tranche can then carry a separate coupon priced at a spread off of Treasuries with the same maturity.

The CMO concept needed to be tested in the market. The treasurer of Freddie Mac, Marcia Myerberg, agreed to take the risks and issue the first CMO. It proved successful and achieved acceptance in the marketplace. Of course, we all took victory laps, with the typical amount of Wall Street crowing, and debated about who thought of the concept first. The CMO concept changed the nature of the mortgage securities market. It enabled Wall Street to absorb the full weight of the burden caused by the decline of the thrifts and distribute it to investors over the maturity spectrum at prices across the yield curve.

Although CMOs provided solutions to many of the early problems in the securitization market, it also created new tax problems. The Treasury permitted the use of the grantor trust concept in mortgage-backed securities but only if the grantor trusts were totally passive. The Treasury's worst nightmare was seeing Wall Street firms carving up mortgages and actively managing the results. The Treasury, therefore, restricted the types of CMOs to three-tranche issues. This proved to be excruciatingly simplistic and expensive, but the market accepted it because it had no alternative.

In 1981, I realized that we needed to bring to final resolution the two sets of long-term problems that were stunting the mortgage market: the tax problem and the legal investment problem that the agencies had not resolved completely. I needed to take the legislative route and convince Congress to adopt legislation permitting the capital markets to meet the nation's housing needs more efficiently and effectively. I enlisted some help, Shannon Fairbanks from the White House and Bernie Carl, a respected Washington lawyer. We developed two pieces of proposed legislation: the Secondary Mortgage Market Enhancement Act of 1984 (SMMEA), a doing-business bill that would preempt state laws for rated mortgage securities and make them a legal investment for almost all investors; and a new section of the Tax Code, Trust for Investments in Mortgages (TIMS). We spent two and one-half years lobbying for these sister bills. Finally, SMMEA was passed by Congress. Our Act is cited in the "Investment Section" of every mortgage securities issue as the source of the state law preemption.

Unlike SMMEA, our tax bill was not passed by Congress. It was defeated primarily by Andy Furer, an analyst at Treasury, who opposed the bill because he could not determine our intentions. Given that I do not easily accept defeat, my reaction to the Treasury's opposition was to hire Andy Furer. With the assistance of this brilliant tax analyst, we rewrote the previous bill to meet his objections. The bill was finally passed after two more years of lobbying as part of the Tax Reform Act of 1986. Our legislation created a new tax vehicle called Real Estate Mortgage Investment Conduits, commonly called REMICs.

SMMEA solved our investment problems, and the creation of REMICs gave us our own private provision in the Tax Code. We were now in a position to deploy all of the brilliant technology we had developed. The multitranche CMO, bifurcating mortgage cash flows into IOs, POs, inverse floaters, and devices yet to be invented were now all possible market investments. We won total flexibility.

It could not have come at a better time, for the thrifts' fortunes continued to decline. The thrifts that continued to lend shifted to adjustable rate mortgages, leaving still larger pieces of the market to securitized products. Securitization was being called on to carry more of the housing finance burden. The legislative relief from the legal restrictions was critical to making new funds available to homeowners through the capital markets.

Before discussing many of the pitfalls of securitization, we must take a step back and review what securitization means. The goal was to create an investment vehicle to finance housing in which the investor did not have to become a home loan savant. He or she did not have to know very much, if anything, about the underlying mortgages. The structure of the deal was designed to place him or her in a position where, theoretically, the only decisions that had to be made were investment decisions. No credit decisions were necessary. The credit mechanisms were designed to be bulletproof, almost risk-free. The only remaining questions for investors concerned their outlook on interest rates and their preferences on maturities. Securitization starts to break down as a concept when the issuer imposes on the investor the responsibility of analyzing the underlying collateral. In truth, with a mortgage pass-through, you have not created a security in the classic Wall Street sense. You have just taken an ugly object, a home loan, and dressed it up. This was the basis of our thinking whenever we securitized any product.

After a difficult period of trial and error, we had perfected the mortgage product and decided to apply it to many other asset types such as credit cards, auto loans, mobile homes and commercial property mortgage loans. We also exported the concept to the United Kingdom, Australia, New Zealand, and other nations.

It might appear that the growth and development of the mortgage market occurred in a straight line, but we had some spectacular failures. Our major error was that we decided to securitize everything. For example, an early opportunity occurred in second mortgages. When home loan rates hit double-digit levels in the early 1980s, many homeowners took out second mortgages in order to protect their low-rate, fixed-rate first mortgages. We were able to successfully securitize the second mortgages and achieve an investment-grade rating on the securities through the use of private mortgage insurance. This became what appeared to be a very successful product. The business grew, especially through loans from California, until one day I received a phone call from Bill Lacy, of Mortgage Guarantee Insurance Corporation, today its CEO, who said, "Lewis, we have a problem. The borrowers are giving us the keys to the houses at the loan-closing table." "What are you talking about?" I asked. "When we close the second mortgage, guys are coming in and just giving us the keys. They are not even making the first loan payment!" Again I asked: "What are you talking about?" Californians, it seems, are always smarter than we are when it comes to real estate scams. These homeowners were faced with declining property values and were unable to sell their homes at a profit. However, they discovered that if they could get a high enough appraisal, a lender would make them a sufficiently large second mortgage to return their equity. The loans were then sold to us, and we were left with the consequences of the scam. We, in effect, bought houses. Based on this experience, we learned all about the risks in appraisals and appraisers.

Mobile home financing also presented a situation where we were forced to alter our program in response to initial losses. Originally, we failed to recognize two facts about mobile home financing. The first was that security for a loan must include both the shelter unit and the land or lot. Unfortunately, in the case of mobile homes, sometimes our collateral went down the highway, never to be seen again. A second difficult lesson we were forced to learn after purchasing hundreds of millions of dollars of loans was that, unlike single-family detached properties, mobile homes tend to depreciate further than they appreciate. In fact, the lending community actually exacerbates the depreciation by financing everything, including the carpets, furniture, drapes, and dishes.

Because of these flaws in the design of our early mobile home program, we were faced with large losses when we repossessed the mobile homes—assuming we could locate our collateral. Due to our initial experience, we rapidly changed the rules. We decided to work only with loans that included both the land and the homes. We introduced standards applied to the quality of the unit and other factors. Despite these improvements in the program, mobile homes continue to be one of the hardest types of residential housing to securitize.

As a general principle, we found that in order to successfully securitize an asset type, one must be able to predict the actuarial experience of defaults. Single-family homes have an actuarial foundation. This same attribute applies to large pools of auto and credit card loans, as well as to certain pools of commercial loans. However, no one has ever been comfortable securitizing airplane leases. With the first plane crash, the losses would be catastrophic to the entire bond issue. This problem could not be mitigated by insurance because the premium would be prohibitively expensive.

There are several elements that create an actuarial basis for evaluating mortgage assets and serve to enhance credit quality. First, unlike that of corporate bonds, the credit quality of mortgage pass-through securities improves over time. As the loan balance amortizes each month, the loan-to-value ratio declines even if home prices remain stable. If there is any inflation, home prices should rise. This further improves the loan-to-value ratio. Additionally, the credit quality of mortgages of young homebuyers tends to improve over time as their income rises and enhances their ability to service their mortgages.

Many of these factors that gave standard mortgage products high credit quality were missing in new mortgage products we devised. One such product was the graduated payment mortgage (GPM). We developed the GPM with the federal agencies to assist families who could not previously afford home ownership. This product is based on the principle that inflation enables workers to get annual wage increases of 6 percent or more each year. The mortgage was designed with a rising payment schedule that gives credit for these wage increases. Therefore, a lender can qualify a borrower at a low monthly payment today and then step the payment up 6 to 7 percent a year. This enables more households to qualify for mortgages. Unfortunately, following a reasonable market acceptance, the GPM product proved to be a failure. This occurred because we overlooked a fundamental reality: everyone does not succeed. In fact, some of us fail. Most simply get along. Therefore, a pool of GPM loans had default rates well above the actuarially allowable standard of three or four out of a hundred. Furthermore, if pay raises slowed or a recession occurred, defaults could be catastrophic. We learned that structures that depend on people succeeding and earning more each year do not follow the same actuarial trend as traditional mortgage products.

A second new product that suffered from structural flaws was the adjustable rate mortgage (ARM). The early adjustable-rate mortgages, termed "variable-rate mortgages," were first introduced in California. The adjustable-rate mortgages were designed to float with an external market rate or cost-of-funds index. However, when the interest rate index rose, which in turn increased the borrowers' monthly payments, mortgagees protested the payment hike, and many defaulted on their mortgages. In response to the high default rates, the lenders, regulators, and mortgage insurers put caps and collars on adjustable-rate loans. As a result of the payment caps, the mortgages became known as "sinkers" instead of "floaters." When market interest rates rose sharply, the interest-rate adjustments on the ARMs did not keep pace with the market. At certain points they could be so far below the real market rate that the securities would trade like a fixed-rate pool, thereby earning the name sinkers. They floated, but always below water. In my view, the Ginnie Mae ARM, currently being offered in the marketplace, is destined to be the next generation of sinkers.

In addition to problems with the underlying collateral, we also faced difficulties developing structures and forms of credit enhancement for the new securities. An important lesson was that all credit mechanisms are not created equal. Historically, we had used the junior-senior subordinated structure for credit enhancement. We began using bank letters of credit in place of the junior-senior subordinated structure because letters of credit were cost efficient and easy to obtain. However, we learned that letters of credit were a very different credit enhancement mechanism than any we had used before. The letter of credit is only as good as the issuing organization. Every time a bank's credit rating was downgraded, the mortgage securities supported by its letter of credit were also downgraded. Who could have ever believed that the rating of the mighty Citicorp and the Japanese banks would be downgraded? Suddenly, we wound up with single-A mortgage securities in a market where we taught investors not to think about credit. Our sales premise, that all credits are created equal, suddenly was no longer true.

The securitization adventure was not without its dark side. Since this topic is not addressed often, it is important that it is included in this report. When testifying before Congressional committees on the REMIC legislation, I was asked how much that legislation would save homebuyers. I opined that the savings would be at least seventy-five basis points per year. Based on average originations of $700 billion a year, that would amount to over $5 billion of savings per year. In fact, the entire securitization process, which I believe has reduced the cost of mortgage funds by two hundred basis points from the presecuritization days, saves borrowers $14 billion per year. However, the costs of securitization have been great.

Securitization contributed to the bankrupting of the thrift industry. The federal government started the process in the late 1970s by deregulating financial institutions. The removal of Regulation Q and the ceilings on savings deposits in the late 1970s left thrifts with mismatched thirty-year, fixed-rate loans. Wall Street, through securitization, finished the job by taking away the thrifts' primary business of home lending. In the United States, the process of deregulating financial institutions has been mismanaged. This mismanagement will ultimately cost the American taxpayers about $500 billion. To date, it is not clear whether the interest savings to homeowners has exceeded the costs of the so-called thrift bailout.

Interestingly, the experience in the United Kingdom was very different. Its financial leadership learned a great deal from our experience. When their thrift system, the building societies, were subjected to deregulation and the competition of securitization, the Ministry of Finance made a ruling that a securitized mortgage instrument was a weaker credit than a whole loan. Despite the international Basle Accord of world bankers, which gave securities with liquidity a higher credit standing than individual loans, in the United Kingdom a mortgage security with credit enhancement has a greater capital charge than individual loans without it. The British were unwilling to allow securitization to destabilize their thrift system. They understood that securitization had come of age but felt that a transition was necessary. They would not allow it to be a blunderbuss and destroy good with bad. Unfortunately, no such wisdom affected our politically charged financial restructuring.

A final topic to address is an important structural change that threatens the viability of the mortgage securities market. This structural change involves the elimination of the call protection embedded in mortgages. Without call protection the mortgage instrument becomes so perfect for the borrower that a large economic benefit is taken away from the other participants, including the long-term investor. When we first created mortgage pass-through instruments, we were able to give the investor de facto call protection because of the way the mortgage origination process worked. A homeowner could not successfully refinance a home loan without incurring front-end costs of 2 percent. These include loan points, application fees, appraisal fees, title fees, and other charges. In addition, mortgage bankers and thrifts were reluctant to do market refinancings because it could result in lost servicing income.

Today, with mortgage bankers originating over 50 percent of all home loans and correspondent loan systems emphasizing new origination volume, competition has virtually eliminated the up-front loan points and significantly reduced other costs. It is now economically advantageous for borrowers to refinance loans when home loan rates decline by as little as twenty-five basis points. The de facto call protection has disappeared. For the time being, the extra money has gone to the refinancing borrower, but the effect on housing finance promises that a day of reckoning lies ahead. This is demonstrated in the Black-Scholes model. This model demonstrates that investors will require a wider interest rate spread on securities to compensate them for greater call risk. For example, if interest rates decline by twenty-five basis points, the borrower will refinance and the loan will be called away from the investor. Likewise, if interest rates rise, the duration of the security increases. The investor loses in both situations. Therefore, with the elimination of the embedded call protection, mortgage rates must rise. These structural shifts have changed and perhaps even broken the market.

We have damaged the basic structure of the new housing finance system. We did not build this system to finance refinancing. We built this system to finance housing. Homebuyers of the future will pay the price of this silliness. The effect of an embedded call on the value of CMO securities and the volatility of IOs, POs, inverse floaters, and other derivatives has already taken its toll on financial and corporate balance sheets. Yet, most market participants choose not to pay attention to the results of their individual actions. It is time to go back and fix the system.

4   The Securitization of Commercial Property Debt

Steven P. Baum

Reflecting on the growth of securitization in its initial market, residential mortgage finance, one might conclude that one day it sprang up full-grown. Having joined Salomon Brothers' mortgage staff in 1979, I testify that it took a tremendous amount of work, innumerable experiments with technology, the changing of laws, the education of investors, and a whole series of trial-and-error experiences to launch this financial innovation. The residential securities market could not be termed smoothly operating until probably the mid-1980s.

In my view, the commercial property securitization market today is really still on page 2 of that development book. Although commercial property securities prototypes have been around since the mid-1980s, those efforts suffered from several deficiencies. First, the rate of return or price investors wanted for taking such risks and the costs of creating the necessary instruments to get the risk to them in acceptable form was well above what direct lenders, insurance companies and banks, would charge. Competition from tax shelter syndicators also limited the market. In the 1980s Wall Street was underbid when it attempted to securitize commercial property loans. As a general principle, where direct lenders, especially major institutions, make ample funds available to a market, be it residential or commercial, these primary lenders are almost always going to win out over securitization.

Second, there was no real investor acceptance of the commercial securitized product. No new investor group that would buy our credit-enhancement premise appeared. To a large extent the securities that were sold were purchased by lenders who were already direct investors in commercial real estate. They might buy the double-A-rated bond that Salomon created, but they did not stop their credit analysis there. They would go out and look at the property anyway. "We're really making a real estate loan. You can't fool us, Wall Street," was their message.

Conditions changed after 1989, owing primarily to one force: the crash of real estate values and the resulting sudden surplus of real estate assets. Throw in the demise of the thrifts and the changes in federal tax laws regarding real estate, and you created a huge crisis of funding in commercial property markets. The traditional sources of funds—insurance companies, banks, thrifts—were unable to continue to support the market because of earlier losses, regulatory changes, and the public perception problems. If you are Citibank and every day in the business press you are reading about your commercial real estate problems, it becomes difficult to go out and make more loans—even if your directors would let you. Furthermore, you had this huge new company formed—the Resolution Trust Corporation (RTC)—which found itself the owner of a tremendous block of real estate assets inherited from failed thrifts. A good portion of these assets were multifamily and commercial real estate loans. Although the RTC found it could move single-family risks off its books efficiently thanks to the securitization markets that had been developed in these fields, what to do on the multifamily and commercial side was unclear.

The agency officials and their advisers debated whether simply to hold auctions and sell to the highest bidder, or to try to develop some type of securitized instruments that would move loans and properties off its balance sheet in bulk. They did some of each. Auctions typically involved the worst assets—mortgages in extended default, for example. Such assets sold at quite severe discounts, again, in large part because of the lack of capital to support commercial real estate markets. When it came to performing loans, albeit highly leveraged performing loans, it did not seem the best strategy to auction these at seventy to eighty cents on the dollar, so a securitization program was developed. The RTC decided to create securities out of mortgage pools and provide first-loss guarantees—cash reserves and federal guarantees—against these pools in sufficient quantity to gain a double-A or triple-A rating from the rating agencies. On the basis of these guarantees, public investors outside the real estate investor market were enticed to provide funds to the RTC. The level of guarantees offered initially were extremely high, ranging between 25 and 50 percent. The RTC, because it held so many assets, was also able to create large pools and diversify the risks in any one pool geographically and by type of asset. This combination of elements gave investors the courage to commit funds to the risk, even though there was no historical or actuarial basis for evaluating the risk.

Investors' thought processes went as follows: "This is a structure I can believe in. With this size first-loss protection, this is equivalent to a double-A or triple-A bond. Yes, I'm going to read the prospectus and worry a bit about the credit aspects of the deal, but the credit enhancement keeps me far from any losses. So, this is a double-A or triple-A that gives me a significant yield pick-up relative to any comparable security. Let's buy it!" In my view, when you start a new market or launch a new product in the capital markets, you certainly price it to sell. The RTC securities were priced to sell.

This RTC effort had a very important effect on the future development of commercial real estate securitization. For the first time Wall Street had attracted bond investors who did not consider themselves specialists in commercial real estate lending as buyers of real estate securities. It had tapped a new funding source at a time when there was a vacuum to be filled.

In my experience, securitization was born to a greater extent out of a need for capital than out of the desire for a lower price of capital. Its ability to make capital available at a time of funds shortages provided the impetus for its expansion into new fields. Nowhere is this more true than in the commercial real estate markets. This is the hot area in the mid-1990s because of the disastrous conditions of the late 1980s and the withdrawal of traditional funding sources from the market.

Commercial real estate mortgages present a panoply of unique challenges to those seeking to securitize such assets and offer them for sale in the public capital markets. When securitizing home loans, car loans, credit cards, or other broadly generated, homogeneous debt instruments, the underwriter can rely on an actuarial-type experience that flows from the law of large numbers. With home loans, for example, based on historic experience over business cycles and depressions, the analyst can see that normal losses might be 2 percent, or 2 out of 100 cases. Recessions and depressions can run losses up to three or five times normal losses. So, given a salvage value of 60 percent or more, a first-loss guarantee of 5 percent of the pool assets will nearly remove the credit risk from the deal. You can have confidence that you have a double-A or triple-A security. In fact, if a mortgage insurer or letter of credit is the source of the enhancement, you shift your credit analysis to a study of the financial strength of that guarantor. Pools of car loans or credit card loans would be subject to a similar model.

What you have to worry about and price in these deals is, not credit risk, but the timing of cash flows and durations.

In the market in which I now work, the commercial mortgage-backed securities market, the exact opposite is true. The beginning and end of the process by which we create commercial mortgage securities is in credit analysis and its development. Unlike the residential market, the commercial market does not have uniformity of mortgage instruments, standardization of underwriting procedures, reliable statistics on historical experience, or the power of government guarantees. In fact, I wish we had even one of the four, much less all four. In truth, we are unlikely to get them. The highly desirable standardization is not possible because the assets themselves are unique. Those people serving the commercial real estate market operate in a private sector field that has job-order, custom deal features. To date, we have not enjoyed the unifying benefits of governmental agency underwriting standards, preemptions, or guarantees. Thus, in structuring deals we are forced to focus on credit-tranche bifurcation rather than cash flow timing structures to attract investors and to protect their principal.

The volume in the commercial mortgage-backed market in 1993 was $20 billion, up from about zero in 1990. Given that the commercial real estate market is much smaller than the residential mortgage market and the car or credit card markets, that volume is a good beginning. Securitization is filling a funding vacuum at a time of need, helping to bring us out of the real estate depression and protecting the values behind many life insurance policies and pension annuities. Equally important, by helping to clear the market of distressed properties, it is encouraging the revival of new lending. Over the longer term, I envision the commercial mortgage-backed market's accounting for perhaps 25 percent of total market activity. Insurance companies and banks, despite regulatory constraints, will come back into the market but will have to share it with Wall Street as it creates real estate investment trusts and other securitized vehicles.

The more restrictive capital standards placed on insurance companies and banks regarding commercial real estate lending are favoring the growth of securitization. The new risk-based capital rules generally have made it a great deal more expensive to hold commercial whole loans than rated securities. Because of the capital differential, you see major institutions and many smaller ones securitizing large pieces of their mortgage portfolios to obtain regulatory relief. They may sell off the junior-most pieces but put the balance of the securities back into their investment holdings. Instead of holding $1 billion of whole loans at a 3 percent capital charge, they now hold $900 million of investment-grade securities at a .3 percent capital charge.

Now, to technology: How, at this early stage in its development, does this market work? The fundamental building block of the commercial mortgage-backed securities market is credit tranching. A typical deal will have what might be termed a "waterfall of credit classes," each with different priorities to the projected cash flows. A structure with five or more classes would be the usual, with the senior tranche rated triple-A. The next class might be rated double-A, followed by triple-B, double-B, and unrated pieces. You may also have a little excess interest. That will become what is called an XP class. Because it is a little different from its residential counterpart, we do not wish to call it an IO. To date, this is the extent of the structuring one sees in commercial mortgage securities. The cash flow fanciness found in residential markets, with IOs, POs, and inverse floaters does not exist here. Credit tranching is subject to more limits than cash flow tranching. The underlying mortgage instruments incorporate much more stringent call protection and more defined pay down schedules. Thus, cash flow timing is more certain.

The investor's focus of necessity shifts to credit considerations, especially as one moves down the rating scale. The role of the rating agencies—Moody's, Standard and Poor's, Fitch, and Duff and Phelps—is immensely important and cannot be overemphasized. They are the gatekeepers of quality. To the extent that there are standards in underwriting in this field, they come from the rating agencies. Without their participation, the commercial mortgage-backed market might not exist. It certainly would be much smaller in size. The rating agency concern is clearly that the top-rated classes be very, very safe. They view their job as protecting investors in high, investment-grade securities. If something happens to the below-investment-grade or unrated bonds, it is caveat emptor. These classes were sold with higher yields and the associated risks.

To illustrate pricing, let us take the case of a real estate borrower with a high-risk profile seeking to securitize a highly leveraged transaction in mid 1994. The triple-A, seven-year, commercial mortgage–backed tranche would be priced at around 100 basis points off the Treasury curve, the double-A tranche 120 basis points off the curve, triple-B 200 off, and double-B 400 basis points off. By class of security, the price increases are geometric. As to the unrated tranche, one can no longer talk in terms of basis points off the curve. Rather, one talks in terms of a percentage, like 15 percent or 20 percent, depending on the risk profile. So, if a borrower needs a great deal of leverage, the price on the unrated piece, even if it is 5 or 10 percent of the total offering, can add 100 basis points to the overall cost of funds. In cases where such structures are used, it is likely to be because it is the only alternative. And, if it is the only alternative, it is also the best.

Overall, there have been relatively few blowups in the asset securitization markets, especially considering the volume of total issuances over the past fifteen years. Admittedly, however, some of the better known failures have been in the commercial mortgage-backed market. Most notable were the Olympia-York failures in New York City properties.

The role of the rating agencies as surrogate underwriters for the market is extensive. It includes not only the obvious, "Can the guy pay the rent?" assessment and the underwriting of the regional economy but also the huge issue of environmental problems. If an environmental problem exists on a property, and you hold the mortgage, you may not be able to foreclose because the liability that goes with the property is greater than the value of the property. Environmental questions are a big issue, along with engineering issues—the structural integrity of the building, deferred maintenance, what needs to be done to bring this building up to code and modernize it—legal issues, and rights under bankruptcy. Real estate borrowers will try all possible legal remedies to avoid losing a property. So appropriate, albeit complex, legal structuring at the outset is essential to the success of the pool over its investment life. The rating agencies oversee all these aspects of the deal as they approve the bundle of rights and responsibilities that become a commercial mortgage security. In the view of those of us seeking to develop this market, they have set very high standards. Only time will tell whether they are high enough.

One further contrast between the residential and commercial markets should be noted. Residential securitization has a cookie-cutter quality to it. Deal after deal follows the same structure. Commercial market deals are more different from one another than similar. This is true in large part because the types of assets being pooled in themselves have very, very different credit characteristics. The assets can range from apartment, retail, office, and warehouse properties to hotel, resort, factory and nursing home properties. For an apartment property, overall market demographics are important. What are rental rates and trends? What is occupancy in the area? Are you on the right side of the tracks? Is competing product in the pipeline? All such questions are important, but the specific leases with individual tenants are unimportant. In evaluating an office building and certain retail properties, the opposite is true. The credit quality of the large tenants and the expiration dates of their leases can be critical. In office securitizations, individual buildings considered for inclusion in pools are likely to be large, $15 to $20 million each or much more, and significant to the performance of the pool. This is not true in the single-family, auto, or credit card fields, where any one underlying property or contract is not statistically significant to actuarial success.

Another consideration is the source of the properties placed into the securitized pool. Where is the product coming from? Is it the real estate portfolio of a single developer or borrower? Are you being asked to securitize all the properties for DeBartolo, Simon or Taubman? If so, you have added a concentration of risk and a managerial risk component to your exposure. By contrast, you may be able to get cross-collateralization from a single borrower whereby it pledges the equity in all its properties to support the securitization. This becomes particularly attractive to the buyers of the lower rated securities. Now you are underwriting the borrower-manager as much as the properties being pooled. If the transaction consists of a twenty-mall property pool with twenty different borrowers, such considerations would not enter the equation. In the commercial market, the risk profiles and required underwriting can vary deal by deal even for the same property type.

From the investors' perspective, if they invest in the lower rated tranches of a single borrower pool, it becomes pretty much of an on/off switch type of exposure. They are either going to get paid all the money due, or they are in deep trouble and, as junior debtholders, probably face a protracted bankruptcy workout. In a multiborrower pool, the odds that one property asset will go bad are pretty good. One commercial borrower will not make it. So the probability of suffering a loss is higher, but the severity of the loss is likely to be much smaller as compared to the case of a single borrower pool. As an investor, you have to understand the differences between the commercial and the residential real estate securities markets. In the residential field, investors learned they could largely ignore credit risk issues and focus on duration and interest rate risk. In the commercial field, even though you use the rating agencies as surrogate underwriters and give weight to their ratings, credit exposure is still very, very much alive in the various tranches, and appropriate credit analysis is critical to successful investing.

Who is active in commercial real estate securitization today? The sellers fall into two categories. The first group is financial institutions (and you can include the federal government, e.g., RTC and FDIC, here) who are owners of mortgages that were made some time ago and that they want strongly to sell. The second group is real estate borrowers seeking to borrow funds on new investments or to refinance existing properties. With the first you are dealing with preexisting mortgages that you cannot restructure. You must accept whatever documents they are written on. You may or may not receive call protection or expense escalation. They are what they are, and your task is to create a security around them. With the second you are working with a developer or owner to create a borrowing form acceptable to the rating agencies and investors at a fair price.

Markets in 1994 continue to be dominated by restructuring transactions whereby the RTC and FDIC, or large institutions like Bank of America and Travelers, seek to securitize big blocks of existing mortgage loans, some of which may be in various stages of distress. We continue to clean out the stables, so to speak, with deliberate speed. Looking ahead, I predict the RTC and FDIC will wind down, and insurance companies and banks will have liquefied all the assets they want to. At that point, if the commercial securitization concept is to continue, it will have to move to the business of providing capital to borrowers who are in the business of buying and building real properties. That process is underway through real estate investment trusts (REITs).

A REIT is a creation of the federal tax code that permits an entity to manage actively real properties and mortgage portfolios for third-party public investors without incurring any tax on transfers of profits to holders of beneficial interest, provided certain conditions are met. The most notable of these is that 95 percent of any net rental, interest, or other income is paid out to investors each year. It is basically a pass-through vehicle like a REMIC, albeit with its own peculiarities. REITs are a specialized form of securitization. Since 1991 there has been an explosion of new offerings of so-called equity REITs, entities that actually own properties and sell stock or shares of that ownership to public investors. Given the new conservatism that has visited the commercial real estate field, REITs, with leverage levels of 20 to 30 percent, fit in very well. Today's markets find such real estate investments attractive, and REIT-related product volume is growing. A review of their securitized borrowings is equally conservative, with few tranches below single-A or triple-B.

Another emerging development deserving note is the creation of commercial mortgage conduits. Even though I am skeptical of their long-term viability, some Wall Street firms have taken upon themselves the creation of commercial mortgage conduits. These are really fledgling credit companies specializing in pooling and passing commercial mortgage risk to the investor market. Given the shortage of funding sources for small and medium-size real estate projects in many cities across the nation, Wall Street is opportunistically stepping up to the plate. The objective is to enable smaller real estate borrowers, those creating $1 to $10 million mortgages, to access the capital markets. Working through a correspondent-originator network, the firms assemble loans into pools for structuring and sale to investors. The credit underwriting takes place at the Wall Street firm. This is why I feel the current commercial conduit model will be short lived. Wall Street's expertise is not in local or regional property underwriting. Our expertise is in structuring, financing, and finding investors.

In the not-too-distant future, another model of commercial mortgage conduit will offer its services to the market. You will see credit companies that fund themselves through securitization rather than through commercial paper and bank lines active in commercial real estate. They will become the ultimate investors in the unrated tranches. In other words, their capital will be the unrated tranches. They will be specialists who are in the business of originating and underwriting the conduit loans to their own standards.

Looking forward, I believe the securitization of commercial real estate will continue to grow. The traditional lenders, insurance companies and banks, will return to the market, but they will not dominate the market as in the past. Pricing of commercial mortgage risk is now linked to the nation's capital markets. The structuring of loans to take advantage of differentials in the yield curve and the liquidity made possible through the ability to trade highly rated tranches will keep Wall Street competitive with portfolio lenders. Real estate investment trusts, now well into a new phase in their history, are likely to contribute significant capital and liquidity to commercial real estate. Commercial mortgage conduits sponsored by well-capitalized credit companies are also likely to bring capital to smaller borrowers across the nation. Finally, in time, we may even see securitization concepts employed in commercial real estate markets globally. The moving force there, as it has been elsewhere, will be a vacuum of available funds to support marketable credits.

5

How Public Corporations Use Securitization in Meeting Financial Needs: The Case of Chrysler Financial Corporation

Dennis M. Cantwell

To help meet its funding needs, Chrysler Financial Corporation (CFC) has used sales of receivables and securitization since 1970. Today we are one of the largest issuers of asset-backed securities. In what follows, I will discuss CFC and its funding, how securitization has evolved at CFC, the two primary kinds of receivables that we have and how we securitize them, the benefits of securitization, and the future of securitization.

As of the end of 1993, Chrysler Financial Corporation managed about $28 billion in finance receivables, most of them auto related. This was done with a balance sheet that had total assets of about half that amount. Shareholder's equity of about $3 billion and very little debt on the balance sheet results in a debt-equity ratio of less than three to one (see table 5.1). This is a very unusual capital structure for a finance company. But a lot of history has led CFC to where it is today—a $28 billion company with a $14 billion balance sheet. The reason for this is securitization, plain and simple.

Like any finance company, CFC can fund itself using a variety of sources. First, we can borrow the money. For the short-term, we can issue commercial paper. It is relatively easy to get into the commercial paper market. Some systems and a small staff are needed—CFC has only two people. Or, an agent like Goldman Sachs or Merrill Lynch can be used. Backup lines of financing from banks are needed, and an investment-grade rating and a recognizable name with a good reputation help a lot. But that is about it. Alternatively, we can borrow from banks under either committed lines or informal lines. We can issue long-term debt in the public or private markets. Here, too, it helps to have an investment-grade rating, though from time to time junk bonds are available for non-investment-grade finance companies. Another option is medium-term notes, largely an investment-grade market. You might go to the European markets for term debt. These

Table 5.1
Chrysler Financial Corporation selected financial data ($ millions)

	1989	1990	1991	1992	1993
Receivables managed	35,411	35,826	33,706	30,138	28,262
Total assets	30,090	24,702	21,280	17,548	14,402
Common equity	2383	2504	2767	2998	3131
After-tax earnings	284	313	276	231	129
Debt-to-equity	8.78	6.71	5.34	3.92	2.69
Fixed charge coverage	1.17	1.23	1.27	1.28	1.31

alternatives—the debt part of the financing of your company—are pretty straightforward. Registration statements are needed, certain disclosures must be made, and certain reporting requirements must be satisfied.

Compared with these more traditional debt alternatives, securitization takes more documentation, more rating agency scrutiny, and more legal and tax involvement on every issue. Auditors are involved more. There are more trustees, sometimes more than one trustee on a single transaction. Special computer systems are needed to do the analysis and to monitor the securitizations. Sometimes, daily reporting to the trustees is required. And to top it all off, securitization is an area of finance that is still evolving. New problems and controversies seem to arise every week. Just about the time when you thought you had it down pretty well, someone—the accountants, the lawyers, the courts, or the Securities and Exchange Commission (SEC)—does something to change things. Even so, CFC still chooses to do a lot of securitization.

Chrysler Financial uses two teams of people to do securitizations, an internal team and an external team. Internally, CFC has three or four people in corporate finance who work on securitizations. They are supported by a few people in the general counsel's office, a few analysts and programmers in management information systems, and some accountants and tax experts who do the required analysis and reporting. There are also operations and credit people who extend the credit, run the branches, and do the analysis on the asset side of the balance sheet. These are the people who meet with the rating agencies for the due diligence that is such an important part of the securitization structuring process.

Externally, there is a larger team, and CFC uses this team perhaps differently than other issuers. The structuring underwriter designs the securitization for CFC. We at CFC have ideas, and we have objectives. But the underwriters have the computers, the mathematics Ph.D.'s who do most of the modeling, and the broad view of the market that CFC does not have. Instead, CFC looks for innovation from Wall Street and has been very successful in getting it. The underwriting syndicate does the pricing and selling of the securities. Although CFC uses in-house counsel for our own legal work, our underwriters' counsel does the documentation. Usually, all four rating agencies—Standard and Poor's, Moody's, Fitch, and Duff and Phelps—are asked to rate the issue. They test and stress the structures and finally rate them. Independent auditors, trustees, trustees' counsel, and a financial printer complete the team.

Isn't this internal and external infrastructure also needed to issue debt? Yes, but not nearly to the same extent as it is needed for securitization. Why then would a firm want to finance with securitization? Let us look at some history.

In 1970 Penn Central went bankrupt and left the commercial paper market in a shambles. Any firm perceived to be the least bit weak was a real problem for investors. And Chrysler was one of those. So almost without warning, Chrysler Financial lost its access to the commercial paper market. CFC did not lose its credit ratings, but it did lose its investors. That incident sent Chrysler executives all over the country looking for money from banks. But it also prompted the first sales of receivables, and Chrysler Financial has continued to sell receivables, in varying amounts, ever since. Ten years later, in 1980–81, our debt was rated CCC—right on the edge of default—and we were unable to borrow anything from anyone in any market. This was the era of the infamous Chrysler Loan Guarantee Act and Chrysler Financial's Debt Override Agreement. CFC was frozen. Not only were we unable to borrow money, we could not repay it. All of CFC's privately held debt had to remain outstanding so that no claimholders were advantaged over others. CFC could sell receivables, though, and we did—hundreds of millions of dollars of receivables.

Cumulatively, from 1970 through 1988, Chrysler Financial sold over $22 billion of receivables, including our first real securitization transactions beginning in 1986. By the end of 1988, CFC had a funding mix that included 40 percent term debt, 30 percent commercial paper, and 15 percent securitization (see figure 5.1). The company was in good shape in 1988, and this is a funding mix typical of that time.

Starting from this financing mix in 1989, CFC sold receivables to banks but did no public securitizations during the entire year. CFC

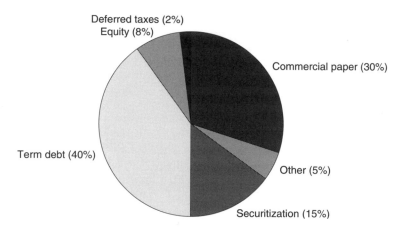

Figure 5.1
Chrysler financial funding sources, December 31, 1988

was an investment-grade company and was perceived favorably in the markets. But then CFC's ratings started to slip again. In December 1989, Moody's reduced our rating from Baa1 to Baa2. Six months later, in June 1990, Standard & Poor's also downgraded CFC. For the next two and a half years, until December 1992, CFC issued no new term debt. Every dollar of funding during that period came from the securitization and sale of receivables and from bank borrowings. By the end of 1993 CFC had begun to recover and was back in the debt markets. But by that time CFC had securitized $65 billion dollars of receivables. On top of that, another $3.5 billion was done in early 1994.

The early 1990s saw some notable milestones in CFC's securitizations. The first wholesale auto securitization took place in 1990, the first wholesale master trust was used in 1991, and CFC's current structure of choice, the Premier Auto Trust, was first used in 1992.

By the end of 1992, securitization accounted for 43 percent of CFC's funding, and bank borrowing accounted for 19 percent. In December 1992 CFC had just returned to the debt market and issued $400 million of new term debt, but figure 5.2 shows how term debt had shrunk as a funding source, from 40 percent of our funding down to 18 percent. Commercial paper was almost nonexistent at this time. CFC was still a non-investment-grade company.

A year later, at the end of 1993, CFC had full access to the capital markets. Commercial paper accounted for 9 percent of CFC's funding, and term debt had grown a little. Securitization, though, accounted for more than half of CFC's funding (see figure 5.3). That funding mix continues today.

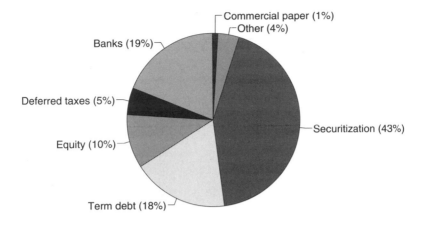

Figure 5.2
Chrysler financial funding sources, December 31, 1992

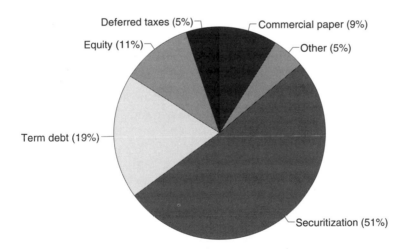

Figure 5.3
Chrysler financial funding sources, December 31, 1993

This has been a brief history of the financing side of our balance sheet. Now let us turn to the automotive financing business, and how CFC securitizes it. CFC has two primary lines of business. First, wholesale financing provides dealers the funds to hold inventories of vehicles for sale: mostly new cars and trucks, sometimes used cars and trucks. The other line of business is retail financing, provided for consumers to purchase these vehicles.

First, consider the wholesale business. Dealers sell cars every day. The dealers pay for the cars when they sell them, and then they are advanced more money to buy new cars. So there is buying and selling and cash flow virtually every day, a system somewhat like that of a credit card. As with a credit card, there are advances every day. Where a credit card requires a single payment each month, however, the dealers pay every day. That daily payment becomes significant in determining how the securitizations are structured.

CFC finances about 75 percent of all of Chrysler's auto sales to the dealers—more than $6.6 billion at the end of 1993. The loans to the dealers are secured and turn over quickly. The payment rate per month is anywhere from 30 percent to more than 50 percent of what the dealer has on the lot. So it involves tremendous cash flows. The dealers are charged a floating rate of interest that may be anywhere from 0.5 percent to 2 percent over the prime rate. In the 1980s CFC financed this with commercial paper and had bank backup facilities to manage that. Today, CFC has $2 billion to $2.5 billion of commercial paper, and the rest of the funding is provided by securitization.

As mentioned above, the cash flows behave like those of credit cards, and CFC securitizes them like credit card receivables. Currently, a master trust structure that was originally developed by the credit card companies is used. (As an aside, I should tell you that we have learned from others, and we are quite willing to adapt or adopt what other people have done. This is far cheaper and easier and faster than trying to reinvent it all.)

The master trust is revolving, with the trust collecting money every day and reinvesting it in new receivables. This is done seamlessly but does require that purchases and redemptions of receivables be reported to the trustees daily. The master trust, as compared with CFC's prior stand-alone trusts, permits the issuance of a number of different securities from a much larger pool of receivables, with the assets in the trust supporting all of the securities. This provides for better diversification. The bankruptcy of a $2 million dealer in a $100 million trust is significant. It is relatively insignificant in a $6 billion trust. This revolving pool provides CFC an opportunity for relatively long-term funding. The longest maturity that CFC has issued so far has been five years, compared to the thirty or forty days provided by commercial paper. The securities are structured with bullet maturities. This minimizes the amortization risk—the risk that the pool pays off and the investors get their money back sooner than expected—and is designed to appeal to investors' preferences. CFC has quite a bit outstanding now, over $4.5 billion as of the end of 1993, with maturities of up to five years. As these securities mature, we plan to replace that funding with new issues from the master trust.

Chrysler Financial still has two wholesale receivable trusts that are separate from the master trust. These date from 1990 when CFC first securitized wholesale receivables. At that time no one had thought of master trusts. Or if someone had, it had not reached the point where they were being used. So CFC did two individual trusts that year. Both were five-year arrangements. Since then, because of the developments in securitization, CFC has gone back to investors to amend some of the terms. Today, the master trust is the tool of choice. We see no reason to use any other kind of securitization for wholesale receivables.

Now let us consider the retail business. Most of this is installment financing. Someone buys a car at a dealer and finances it over forty-eight months. The dealer writes the loan contract and then sells it to a bank, a finance company, or Chrysler Credit. That accounts for most of CFC's retail financing and is the type of receivable we securitize. The remainder is rent-a-car financing and leasing. CFC had a total of about $14 billion in retail managed at the end of 1993. Most of this, about $10 billion, was securitized.

The structure we use for retail is an owners' trust. Unlike wholesale, retail is essentially a static pool. Once the pool is in place, nothing is added to it. The pool amortizes, and the payments pass through to the investors in the various tranches. Both debt and equity securities of the trust are sold. The debt securities account for about 96 percent of the value of the trust, and the equity for about 4 percent. The debt is structured in different tranches, depending on what the market likes at the time. A typical deal might have four different classes of securities: three debt tranches and the equity. One deal that has this structure, Premier Auto Trust 1993-2, is illustrated in figure 5.4. The first debt tranche, A-1, consists of money market notes with a very short maturity. These securities receive the first cash flows in the deal and have an expected maturity of nine months. The next debt tranche, A-2, consists of floating-rate notes with an expected maturity of about twenty-nine months. The last debt tranche, A-3, consists of fixed-rate notes with an expected maturity of forty-five months. Finally, at the bottom, is the equity, called the B certificates. The B certificates amortize with the A-3 tranche.

CFC incorporates a floating-rate tranche only when there is an appetite in the market for floating-rate securities. If there is not a substantial appetite for floating-rate products, deals with only fixed-

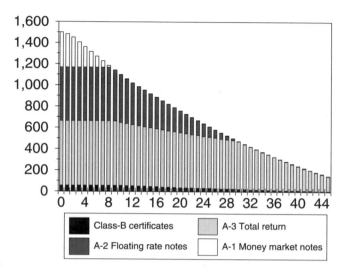

Figure 5.4
Chrysler financial: Premier 1993–2 outstanding principal ($ millions)

rate tranches are offered. Because the receivables are fixed rate, CFC may hedge its floating-rate exposure with caps, either inside or outside the trust, or by undertaking a swap outside the trust. The overall objective, though, is to minimize the cost of funds by structuring the deal so that the securities appeal to the market.

Chrysler Financial uses a shelf registration for retail securitization. This eliminates the need to register each retail securitization and wait for SEC approval. It enables us to go to the market almost within hours. For instance, CFC can decide to go ahead with a retail securitization in the morning, inform the underwriters in the afternoon, and have the deal priced the next day. That could mean $1.5 billion of financing in less than twenty-four hours. That is the power of a shelf registration statement and, by the way, of securitization generally. One more point to note is that unlike Gallo, who say they will sell no wine before its time, CFC does sell receivables even before they are originated. This is called prefunding. We can do it because CFC has the necessary credibility as well as the capability to predict what kind of receivables will go into a trust. Prefunding enables CFC to take advantage of good markets when they are there.

Those are CFC's two types of assets and two types of securitization—the wholesale business with a type of credit card master trust structure; and the retail business with the owners' trust structure.

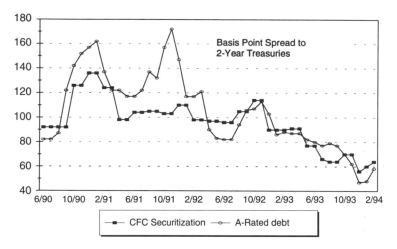

Figure 5.5
Spread comparison: Securitization versus A-rated debt

These securitizations entail substantial overhead, accounting and legal expertise, rating agencies, systems, and more. Nevertheless, the benefits more than compensate for these costs. First and foremost, securitization provides funding at a very attractive price. Figure 5.5 compares the cost of securitization with a two-year average life to the cost of two-year, A-rated debt (measuring each by its basis point spread to two-year Treasury securities). Two things are notable. Securitization was generally less expensive than the A-rated debt, and securitization pricing was less volatile.

The second benefit of securitization is that since the cash passes through to the investors as it is received, this provides CFC with matched funding, both in terms of interest rates and in terms of cash flows. The third benefit of securitization is that it facilitates very large transactions. A $1.5 billion transaction is CFC's standard, and GMAC has done even larger transactions than that. Indeed, the market has shown it can absorb $2 billion or more at a time.

In general, CFC uses a market-based approach to financing. It is somewhat like Chrysler's market philosophy. Chrysler wants to design and build cars that people will want to buy, will enjoy driving, and will want to buy again. Chrysler Financial wants to design securities that investors will want to buy. This means securities that perform predictably and trade well. If securities can be designed to meet these objectives, then investors will come back again. And that is critical if an issuer is going to do $10 billion of this every year.

In designing securities, CFC takes account of the fact that different investors have different preferences. Money market tranches appeal to money market funds, floating-rate tranches appeal to financial institutions, particularly banks, and fixed-rate tranches appeal to fixed-income mutual funds and insurance companies. The market sends feedback through the underwriters who have to sell this stuff. The underwriters tell CFC, and CFC responds. Markets are such that the interest in certain types of securities waxes and wanes, depending on interest rates and volatility in the markets. Of course, not all investors are comfortable with asset-backed securities, but in every deal that CFC does there is some significant new investor. To the extent possible, CFC tracks the identity of the ultimate investors. Furthermore, some say that in pricing deals, CFC leaves money on the table. If so, it is probably not more than a basis point or so, and that is part of the cost of keeping the investors happy.

Meeting the objective of investor satisfaction requires continuous improvement. In some respect every transaction has had some innovation that made it a little better than the last. The master trust replaced the stand-alone trust structure. Permitting the trust to hold cash when inventories hit seasonal low points has reduced the chance of early amortization. Because of another innovation, the liquidity necessary to support a money market security is provided within the structure itself, which has significantly improved our all-in costs and has reduced amortization risk.

The list of innovations is even more extensive on the retail side, the most important of which has been the switch from the grantor trust to the owner's trust. A grantor trust is a tax construct. It is governed by Internal Revenue Service rules, and it is essentially passive. Once it is set up, money can only pass through it. The grantor trust cannot invest on its own or have differently structured classes of securities. The key advantage of the owner's trust is that it can be active. Within the trust, many kinds of securities can be structured. So instead of every security holder having a share in the trust—an ownership interest which is what one has in a grantor trust—there are now both debt and equity pieces. Without going through the other key retail innovations, note that each of the innovations, whether "big" or "little," saves CFC money, anywhere from hundreds of thousands of dollars to literally millions of dollars on individual transactions.

Even someone who is confident that securitization will continue to be an important source of financing must be prepared for the possibility that the securitization market will dry up because of some unforeseen event. Although Chrysler Financial faces no funding risks for what is currently on its balance sheet or for what it currently manages, a securitization blowup could impede future business. CFC handles such risks by keeping bank backup lines in place. Currently, CFC backup lines amount to over $6 billion. This covers possible securitization disruptions as well as commercial paper or term-debt disruptions.

To conclude, I offer ten predictions regarding the future of securitization, in no particular order.

1. The market will continue to grow.

2. The number of issuers will continue to increase.

3. The complexity of deals will continue to increase.

4. Accountants, rating agencies, and lawyers will continue to get rich on the bounty provided by securitization. They will help issuers though they will also make issuers' lives difficult by finding more and more problems with what is done.

5. The number of investors who are comfortable with asset-backed securities and the number of portfolios that invest in asset-backed securities will increase.

6. Securitization will not replace debt. At some point the overhead can get prohibitive, and securitization can become more costly than debt.

7. Small securitizations will become efficient. We are already seeing that. This means that some issuers who otherwise would not have access to competitively priced debt will be able to get funding. One need look no further than the mortgage market to see what happens with securitization over a period of time.

8. The number of underwriters and other participants in the market will continue to grow.

9. Chrysler Financial will continue to use securitization in one form or another. Although it may not always be the primary form of funding, it will have a place for a long time to come.

10. The number of jobs connected with securitization is going to grow. Good people are always in demand.

6

The Contributions of the Resolution Trust Corporation to the Securitization Process

Michael Jungman

The Resolution Trust Corporation (RTC) occupies a special place in the development of securitization. Owing to its size and novel mission, the RTC has also been a shaper of the market. In what follows, I will provide some background on the size and scope of the RTC's task and an overview of the RTC's securitization program, including its landmark commercial mortgage securitization program.

Background on the RTC and Overview of the RTC's Securitization Program

Congress created the RTC in 1989 to resolve the crisis resulting from the insolvency of hundreds of federally insured savings and loan associations. Congress gave the RTC multiple mandates: resolve the failed thrifts at the least cost to the U.S. taxpayer; minimize the impact on local real estate markets and on financial markets; and preserve affordable housing. Congress provided for the RTC to complete its task and terminate as a separate agency at the end of 1996. So it was clearly intended that the RTC was not to be an ongoing agency but was to deal with this specific job and then disappear.

Despite what one might read in the newspapers, the RTC's accomplishments have been substantial. It has taken over more than 750 failed savings and loan associations with about $460 billion in total assets (book value). Aside from defense activities, this is one of the biggest undertakings in the history of the federal government.

As of early 1994, the RTC has sold or collected assets with a total book value of $399 billion, recovering $358 billion, about 90 percent of the book value. The RTC has protected more than twenty-two million insured depositors with an average account balance of $9,000. This was accomplished either through payoffs or through transfers of the ac-

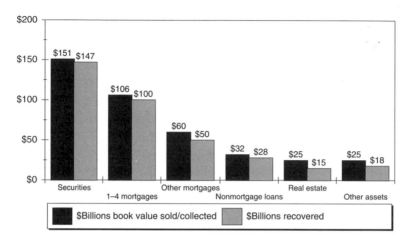

Figure 6.1
Recoveries from sales and collections ($358 billion); 89.7% of book value

counts to other insured institutions. This program has been frequently referred to as a bailout, but it is important to remember that none of the RTC's money went to pay off stockholders, owners, or operators of failed thrifts. Every dollar was spent to protect insured depositors.

The degree of success in recouping the value of the assets taken over from the failed institutions varies, depending on the type of asset. This is illustrated in figure 6.1, which shows how the $399 billion in book value that has been sold and the $358 billion that has been recovered is distributed across asset types. As one would expect, the recovery rate is highest for securities that were held by the failed institutions, $147 billion recovered out of an original book value of $151 billion, or 97 percent. The second highest recovery rate is on one-to-four-family mortgages, where $100 billion out of $106 billion, or 94 percent, has been recovered. The recovery rates are lower on other mortgages, nonmortgage loans, real estate, and the failed institutions' other assets.

The RTC's job is nearly completed. There remains $61 billion of assets. The job might even be finished today but for the change in political administrations. This put a brake on the process in early 1993. In disposing of the remaining assets, the RTC can expect the average recovery rate to drop. This is because the remainder of the portfolio tends to be more real estate and more poor-quality assets. Nevertheless, the overall recovery rate is going to be quite a bit higher than was originally expected.

At the outset, the RTC did not securitize the assets that it sold. Securitization was first used about one year into the program. It was a response to market conditions and a response to the fact that the RTC needed to tap every possible market to liquidate the enormous volume of assets under its control.

In late 1990, the RTC's oversight board directed the agency to initiate a securitization program and create a single entity or procedure to securitize assets coming out of failed institutions. The RTC was authorized to use credit enhancement for the securitizations but not government guarantees. Further, the RTC was encouraged to rely on private-sector expertise, hence experienced private-sector firms were selected to participate in transactions as underwriters, financial advisors, trustees, loan servicers, accountants, and printers. Another element in the securitization program was the use of master swap agreements with Freddie Mac and Fannie Mae. In addition, in February 1991 a special amendment to the Securities Act of 1933 was adopted providing RTC directors and officers with immunity from securities law liabilities. This protection was deemed necessary because of the lack of complete knowledge about many of the assets in the portfolio to be sold.

In March 1991 the RTC filed a shelf registration statement with the Securities and Exchange Commission to offer securities backed by mortgages from any RTC institution. This gave the RTC quick access to the markets on a frequent, regular basis. By late 1991, about six months after the first securitization transaction was completed, the agency was pleased with the program's success and adopted securitization as the primary and priority method of disposing of all performing mortgage loans in the system.

The objectives of the securitization program were to expedite asset sales and increase recovery values. Early on, the RTC had been criticized for moving too slowly. So the RTC set very aggressive sales goals for 1991. As I recall, these goals included the sale of $23 billion of single-family mortgages in 1991. That this was an ambitious goal is underscored by the fact that in the preceding year, the entire whole loan market for single-family mortgages was about $5 billion. To dispose of the huge volume of assets held by the RTC, access to the mortgage-backed securities markets appeared essential.

Selling such an enormous volume of assets quickly and at high prices required a high-quality standardized product that would appeal to a broad investor base. This meant certain changes in the way that the RTC had been operating. For the most part, the RTC had operated its sales programs through a number of regional offices, each with its own procedures. Investors often were frustrated at the lack of a more centralized and predictable process. Securitization was intended as a method of developing a frequent, regularly scheduled offering of a standardized investment product. Buyers could become accustomed to seeing repeated sales of familiar securities. This would enable investors to buy on twenty-four hours notice instead of having to do thirty days worth of due diligence.

Mortgage-backed securities also had the advantage of appealing to a broader investor base. This was at a time when the banks, the remaining thrifts, and the insurance companies were all fleeing the real estate markets. There were few portfolio buyers of mortgage loans. There were, however, a great many buyers of rated securities. So it was a natural strategy to move out of a $3–4 billion a year market and move into a market that provides hundreds of billions of dollars per year. All of these factors—simplified procedures, standardized products, and access to the broad array of investors in the mortgage-backed securities markets—serve to expedite sales and get better pricing.

By early 1994, the RTC had completed about $43 billion of securitization transactions. These transactions ranged across a variety of collateral types. Of this amount, $20.9 billion is accounted for by thirty-five transactions involving single-family mortgages that did not conform to Freddie Mac or Fannie Mae standards. There were eleven multifamily mortgage transactions, totaling $4.5 billion. There were twelve transactions involving mixed pools of commercial and multifamily mortgages, totaling $9.5 billion. The multifamily and commercial mortgage transactions are noteworthy. They represented a significant new development because these were categories of assets that had not been previously sold in the securitization market to any significant degree. There also were four transactions involving mobile home, home-equity, and other loans, totaling $1.1 billion. There were five transactions backed by pools of nonperforming commercial mortgages that totaled $1.6 billion. Finally, there was $5.7 billion of swaps involving conforming one-to-four-family mortgages.

Looking at the program over time, we note that the first transaction was completed in June 1991. This was a $500 million transaction. After that, the RTC began accessing the market on a regular monthly basis. The RTC averaged about $1.9 billion per month through the first quarter of 1993 (a total of twenty-one months). As one can imagine, over this time period the RTC was a popular issuer in the securities markets. During the final three quarters of 1993, however, a total of only $1.2 billion in mortgage-backed securities were issued. Some of us who have left the agency call this the "Clinton effect," reflecting the fact that the new administration came in and basically halted the securitization program, as well as many other aspects of the RTC's activities.

Unlike the motives of other issuers of asset-backed securities, the RTC's motives had nothing to do with accounting treatment or balance sheet management. The RTC's motive was to sell a large volume of assets over a short period of time at a high price. Had the RTC tried to sell that kind of volume in the whole loan market, it would have significantly depressed market prices. Through the securities market, the RTC could get higher prices and hence, better value for taxpayers.

The RTC estimates that, thus far, the securitization program produced roughly $3.4 billion of additional proceeds as compared to whole loan sales. The greatest relative benefits of securitization versus whole loan sales were in multifamily/commercial mortgages because this is where there is the greatest disparity between whole loan pricing and securitization pricing. The RTC's experience indicates that whole loan sales generated prices that amounted to 73.8 percent of book values whereas securitization generated prices that amounted to 92.9 percent of book values. If we assume that the percentages for the actual whole loan sales would have also applied to the assets securitized, then the incremental proceeds on the $9.5 billion of book value equals $1.8 billion. So even though the multifamily/commercial component was a smaller percentage of the total assets securitized, it was a major contributor to the $3.4 billion of additional proceeds. The incremental proceeds on the $20.9 billion of book value on one-to-four family mortgages is estimated to be $1.1 billion. Here the pricing disparity was not as great, 98.5 percent recovery with securitization and 93.2 percent with whole loan sales, but the huge volume of mortgages still led to a significant difference in proceeds. The incremental proceeds on the $4.5 billion of multifamily mortgages is estimated to be $.5 billion, the recovery rates being 94.2 percent with securitization and 83.9 percent with whole loan sales.

RTC Commercial Asset Securitizations

The RTC's commercial asset securitizations represented a significant breakthrough in the market, and the way the product was structured is instructive. Consider the RTC's 1993-C2 transaction, a commercial mortgage securitization. The collateral in this transaction was comprised of 2,514 loans with an aggregate principal balance of about $728 million and an average principal balance of about $289,000. There are both fully amortizing loans (23%) and balloon loans (77%); and there are both fixed-rate loans (46%) and adjustable rate loans (54%). The loans were originated by 237 different originators and are serviced by seventy different servicers. The loans cover all property types: multifamily properties (34%), retail properties (18%), office buildings (17%), with the remainder being a mixture of other property types. The properties are spread across twenty-nine states. This should give a rough sense of the size and diversity of the collateral included in an RTC transaction—it is a large and messy portfolio.

The degree of due diligence required on a commercial asset securitization is much greater than for a residential mortgage securitization. With a pool of a thousand or ten thousand residential mortgages, due diligence can be done on a sampling basis, operating off statistical predictions. For pools of commercial mortgage loans, however, each loan relates to a piece of property on which there is a business, an office building, a warehouse, an apartment building or something else. Due diligence is required to assess a property's prospects for producing income. This will entail the collection of property-level information like rent rolls or operating statements. Such information is important because the earning power of the properties is what drives the rating agency process, and current information from the properties will facilitate the calculation of debt-service coverage ratios. Due diligence can also encompass a number of other things. For instance, it may include tape-to-file verification, meaning that one compares what is in the loan file with what is on the computer tape to see if the two actually match. In many cases, file review or reconstruction is also required. Due diligence might also require visits to properties and physical inspection to evaluate the quality of the real estate. Finally, property inspections may be necessary to be certain that there are no environmental hazards that will cause the trust, and therefore the security holders, to take on liability under the environmental laws. An incidental result of the extensive due diligence is that commercial mortgages is probably the only segment where accountants make more money than investment bankers.

Another difference between residential or asset-backed securitization and commercial mortgage securitization is the servicing. If a homeowner defaults, the consequences are fairly straightforward. Foreclosure follows, and the property is sold. But if the owner of an

apartment building defaults, it is not necessarily the case that foreclosure is optimal. Instead, it may be better for the creditor to restructure
the loan and let the current owner continue operating the apartment
building. This is because the current owner knows the building best
and may be the one who can bring in the greatest future rent revenues.
The problem may not be the owner but the local market. Providing
the servicer with an element of discretion, not present with residential
mortgages, means that these types of loans require much more complex servicing arrangements. Specifically, the servicing functions are
typically split between two firms. One firm, called the master servicer,
performs the normal loan-servicing functions like collections, escrows,
and so on. A second firm, called the special servicer, is responsible for
delinquent loans and other loans that require workout skills. The
special servicer is responsible for modifying loan terms upon default
so as to maximize the present value of the future cash flows. The
special servicer is typically a more entrepreneurial, hard-nosed, and
less institutional kind of firm.

Another distinct feature of a commercial mortgage securitization is
that most of the loans have balloon maturities. Consider RTC 1993-C2.
What is supposed to happen when 77 percent of the pool matures and
there is no market for refinancing? Initially this was a very difficult
issue. The structure has to permit a rollover at the end of the balloon
maturity. The solution was to issue pass-through securities with a
nominal final distribution in thirty years—even though the collateral
might have a weighted-average maturity of ten years. Further, the
servicer is given the ability to roll over loans at maturity and put them
on an amortizing basis out to the full term of the pass-through securities. Then, if borrowers can refinance the loan when the balloon
payment is due, they do so, and they go out of the pool. It appears as
a prepayment to the investor. But if the borrower cannot refinance the
loan, then the servicer can roll over the maturing balloon. In this case,
the extended maturity date must be prior to the final distribution date.
If the property income is sufficient, then loan payments must provide
for full amortization by the extended maturity date. If the property
income is not sufficient, then a new balloon maturity must be specified
or the payments must be reduced to permit full amortization. These
securities do not have a lot of prepayment risk. Instead, they have
extension risk.

The commercial transactions use a variation on the master trust. A
variety of different loan types—loans on various commercial property

types and with various interest-rate characteristics—are put into a single REMIC trust. Then the loans are grouped to back specific classes of securities so that investors can buy the security with the characteristics best suited for them. In RTC 1993-C2, for example, the loans were grouped to form four classes of securities. First, the loans were grouped by multifamily versus nonmultifamily. This is because multifamily-backed securities have special treatment under both the capital rules of financial institution purchasers and the securities laws. The loans were then placed in subgroups depending on their interest rate characteristics. Fixed-rate loans and adjustable-rate loans with floors greater than 7.5 percent were put in one subgroup. Since all of the securities had coupons of 7.5 percent or below, the latter loans could be treated as being fixed rate, for their rates would not go below the 7.5 percent floor. Adjustable-rate loans with floors lower than 7.5 percent were put in the other subgroup. Table 6.1 illustrates the grouping of the loans.

This transaction created fixed-rate, sequential-pay securities that were backed by the fixed-rate and adjustable rate loans with floors above 7.5 percent (for both nonmultifamily and multifamily loans) and floating-rate securities, tied to LIBOR, that were backed by the adjustable-rate loans with floors below 7.5 percent (again for both nonmultifamily and multifamily loans).

For credit enhancement, RTC 1993-C2 had a cash reserve of $166 million (23 percent of the principal). The cash reserves supported all of the classes of securities and were invested in Treasury Bills.

Now, consider the level of credit enhancement provided by the senior-subordinated structure. In a residential or asset-backed securities deal, 8 percent credit support (as a percentage of the principal balance of the pool) would be a sizable credit enhancement. With a commercial deal, however, a triple-A rating will require percentages above 40 percent and sometimes even 50 percent. The rating agencies are quite conservative on these transactions. Table 6.1 shows the credit enhancement provided by the senior-subordinated structure in RTC 1993-C2. There, 86 percent of the loans in the pool would have to default, with a 50 percent loss on each of the defaulting loans, before the double-A-rated securities would suffer a loss. So the senior securities are quite protected, for it would take a real disaster to reach them and cause a loss. The RTC provided what might be called robust credit enhancement through subordination and through cash reserves.

Table 6.1
Classes of securities/loan groups and credit enhancement: RTC 1993-C2

Class of securities	Loan group
Class A1-A/B/C commercial senior fixed-rate sequential pay	1. Nonmultifamily fixed-rate mortgages + ARMs with floors above 7.5%
Class A2 commercial senior LIBOR	2. Nonmultifamily ARMs with floors below 7.5%
Class A3-A/B/C multifamily senior fixed-rate sequential pay	3. Multifamily fixed-rate mortgages + ARMs with floors above 7.5%
Class A4 multifamily senior LIBOR	4. Multifamily ARMs with floors below 7.5%
Classes B/C/D/E commercial fixed-rate mezzanine	Loan groups 1 & 2 + excess cash flow from groups 3 & 4

Credit enhancement

Class	Ratings	$ millions	Credit support (% principal)
A	AAA/AAA	557	46
B	AA/AA	43	40
C	A/A	36	35
D	BBB/BBB	36	30
E	BB/BB	50	23

Notes: A cash reserve of $166 million (23%) supports all classes. At 30% cumulative annual default rate (86% total defaults) and 50% loss severity on each loan, no loss to Class A or B.

A final difference is that these transactions are characterized by very attractive yields relative to other securities of equivalent ratings. Asset-backed securities trade at perhaps 20 or 35 basis points over comparably rated corporate bonds. With commercial mortgage transactions, in 1993 it was not surprising to see spreads of 200 or 300 basis points over comparably rated corporate bonds. Those spreads have narrowed now to 100 or 150 basis points, and one would expect them to narrow further. But there is still a substantial premium for investors that are willing to invest in this type of product.

Interestingly, there is actually a fairly active market for all of the tranches of the commercial deals, including the B-rated or the nonrated securities. This is not the case with residential mortgages or asset-backed securities. This is because there are real estate investors who are looking for near-equity types of yields, and they are prepared to analyze the credit risk in the portfolios of real estate properties and make investments at the nonrated or sub-investment-grade levels.

At the time the RTC started doing these transactions, no one gave any thought to inventing something new, or stimulating the market, or creating a technology that the private sector would use. The RTC was just trying to get the best value for the assets. Somewhere along the way, we looked up and were surprised to see that a lot of commentators were saying that what we were doing was pretty unusual and was in fact stimulating the private sector. The innovative techniques that the RTC developed are now in the process of being used by private-sector issuers.

The Market for Commercial Mortgage Securitization

Where is the market at, and where is the market going? Figure 6.2 shows the size of the market for commercial mortgage securitizations. The market bumped along in the 1980s with an average of $1.4 billion issued per year. In 1990 this was up to $5.6 billion. The volume of new issues in the market continued to grow in 1991 and 1992 with the RTC providing a substantial share. In 1993, while the RTC's sale of these

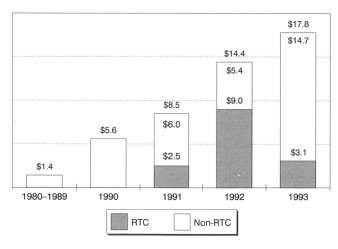

Figure 6.2
The RTC stimulated the commercial mortgage-backed securities market
Source: Commercial Mortgage Alert.

securities dropped, the private-sector almost tripled the volume of its issues.

Growth in the securitized market was occurring at the same time that traditional lenders were getting out of real estate markets. The banks, thrifts, and insurance companies all reduced their real estate exposure during the early 1990s. This was because of losses, regulatory constraints, and the stock market's negative view of institutions that held substantial commercial real estate exposure. As those institutions stepped out of the market, the capital markets stepped in to fill the gap.

By 1993 a diverse group of issuers were tapping the commercial mortgage-backed securities market (see figure 6.3). The RTC accounted for 17 percent of the volume as opposed to 63 percent the year before. The other issuers in 1993 included owners/developers (20%), portfolio buyers (15%), insurance companies (13%), and REITs (11%).

As figure 6.4 shows, a diverse set of underlying property types was brought to market in 1993 as well. Mixed properties accounted for 37 percent of the property securitized. Multifamily properties accounted for 29 percent of the collateral, the largest single component. This popular property type is favored by the rating agencies and investors. There were also substantial numbers of retail properties (17%) and office buildings (8%) in the pool as well.

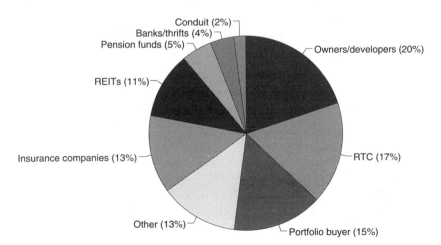

Figure 6.3
1993 saw diverse issuers of commercial mortgage-backed securities
Source: Commercial Mortgage Alert.

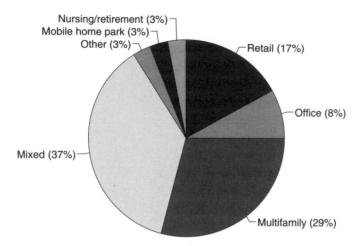

Figure 6.4
1993 saw diverse properties underlying commercial mortgage-backed securities
Source: Commercial Mortgage Alert.

An interesting development in 1993 and 1994 has been the proliferation of commercial mortgage conduits. These conduits are essentially
mortgage companies that originate commercial mortgages for the ex-
press purpose of selling them into the secondary markets. In effect,
they provide small borrowers with direct access to the capital markets.
This is something that has been done for quite a while in the residential
and asset-backed markets. Until now, however, it has not been done
much with commercial properties. I think that this is a development
that is here to stay. Further, I think that it threatens to erode the
position of banks and other traditional commercial real estate lenders
in the same way that securitization has overtaken residential lending.

Commercial mortgage securitization is still very much in its infancy.
The asset-backed securities market is so well developed that you can
raise $1 billion in twenty-four hours. That is definitely not the case in
the commercial area. There, the money can be raised, but the due
diligence and rating process will take three or four months. Then it
takes about two days to actually raise the money.

The market will continue to grow though. Approximately 40 percent
of the $2.8 trillion of single-family mortgages have been securitized.
By contrast, only 10 percent of the $310 billion of multifamily mort-
gages and less than 5 percent of the $755 billion of commercial mort-
gage assets have been securitized. So the product exists, and the
market will continue to grow.

Summary

To summarize, the RTC's contributions to the securitization process fall into three categories. First, the RTC's program helped develop a substantial investor base for commercial mortgage-backed securities. Investors became comfortable with the features of the securities and the kind of analysis necessary. Investors found especially attractive the additional yield that is associated with commercial mortgage securities, concluding that there was not excessive credit risk associated with the securities.

Second, the RTC's efforts allowed the various market participants to develop their analytic technologies at the government's expense. These are very complex transactions. The investors, rating agencies, investment bankers, and lawyers all have a particular technology that had to be adapted for this asset category. The RTC supplied the volume of product and was willing to pay for the development of that technology.

Third, the RTC's efforts helped to return a significant degree of liquidity to a commercial real estate market that had become stagnant. The capital markets are now viewed, perhaps for the first time, as a primary source of debt capacity for commercial real estate. These contributions are highly significant and will benefit the nation's commercial property markets for years to come.

7   The Role of Rating Agencies in the Securitization Process

Neil D. Baron

The place of rating agencies in the nation's capital markets reminds me of the classic movie *Butch Cassidy and the Sundance Kid*. In one memorable scene, Butch and Sundance are looking back at a posse tracking them across impossible terrain, and asking, "Who are these guys?" Many people ask that question about rating agencies. We are always there and getting in the way of an awful lot of transactions. I submit we play a constructive role. Others think that although we are constructive, we are too intrusive.

What do rating agencies do? The major role of rating agencies is to assist investors in making investment decisions. Through research, analysis, and information the nationally recognized credit rating agencies protect investors against unknowingly taking credit risk. Investment grade rating says something very specific. It says a particular instrument will pay interest and principal according to the terms of the indenture. If you hold a twenty-five-year, triple-A bond to maturity, you are assured of getting 100 percent of the principal and interest on a timely basis.

Please note what we do not do. Suppose interest rates rise, and your triple-A mortgage-backed bond drops by 20 percent. Can you sue the rating agency because of your loss? No. That is not credit risk. It is interest rate risk, and credit ratings do not opine on such exposure.

Nor do ratings make any statement about the suitability of a specific investment for a particular investor. Investors have different risk preferences. Some seek out securities that are rated in the lower categories because they are more risk-oriented and want the higher yield. Furthermore, the rating does not make any statement about the appropriateness of the market price of the security. A triple-A-rated security selling at 140 percent of par may be a terrible investment, and a double-B-rated security selling at 60 percent of par could be a terrific investment. It is important to recognize that a rating makes a very precise and limited statement—it opines on the likelihood that payment will be made according to the terms of the indenture.

The services of the rating agency are paid for by the issuer of the securities. Does that not create a conflict of interest that will work to the detriment of the investor? The answer is "No." To explain why, let me tell you the story of the rapid growth of Fitch in the rating field. In 1989, Fitch was the smallest of the four nationally recognized rating agencies, the others being Moody's, Standard and Poor's, and Duff and Phelps. From a staff of 43 we have grown to over 240 employees. In 1989, when we called on investment bankers or issuers, they would say, "We see little need to add another rating to our offerings. You are of no use to us unless investors really believe in your rating and demand it."

The message was clear. Acceptance by investors would be the key to our success. We spent the next two years going around and talking to large institutional purchasers of mortgage- and asset-backed securities. This was a growth field where enhanced analysis could provide greater service. We developed new, more sophisticated analytic tools to enhance the quality of our research. Explaining the proprietary features in how we analyzed different types of securities allowed us to gain the confidence of investors and investment bankers. Making our analysts available directly by phone was also important. In addition, we distributed 90 percent of our research free of charge. Rating agencies earn over 90 percent of their revenues from fees charged to issuers and less than 10 percent from subscription services. We developed and distributed research reports on every single rating that we issued or assigned to a security.

A year and a half later, by December 1990, investors began to call investment bankers and issuers and say, "We'd like to see more Fitch ratings on your transactions." Some would even say, "We don't want to buy it without a Fitch rating." What does this mean? Rating agencies march to the drum of investors because the minute a rating agency begins to appear as though it is accommodating an issuer or banker, a funny thing happens. The pricing of the securities with the ratings of the "captive" agency will begin to deteriorate. Issuers will have to pay a higher interest cost because investors do not have confidence in the rating. Once that happens, issuers will shift quickly to those rating agencies in whom investors have greater confidence.

The track record for agencies as a group has been very good, particularly in the mortgage- and asset-backed securities areas. Even though the thrifts that issued many of these securities failed, to my knowledge there have been no defaults in any highly rated public securities issued by a thrift.

Without ratings, the complex securities in the mortgage field which rely so heavily on the strength of credit enhancements might not be able to be sold. The rating sets a defined credit standard that investors understand and accept. It says the credit enhancement structure is appropriate to the assigned rating. It says the investment decision can now move to consideration of market or interest-rate risk, and duration or maturity risk. This is very important. Securities are traded quickly. There is very little time in the marketing process to permit individual analyses of each deal.

Why else do participants in the capital markets want ratings? Issuers seek ratings because they make their securities more marketable to investors at lower interest costs. As investors gain confidence in the credit analyses of rating agencies, they require a lower yield on an investment. The savings to an issuer can be substantial. And, at times the rating can be the difference between getting money or no money at all. In addition, there are probably over thirty-five different places in federal and state laws and regulations governing the investments of financial institutions where the requirement of ratings are incorporated into regulations. Under the Investment Company Act, for example, taxable money market funds cannot hold more than 5 percent of their assets in securities that are rated lower than the top tier rating categories of two rating agencies. State investment laws for insurance companies and other institutions and funds also typically require ratings to make securities legal investments.

One of the biggest drivers of securitization of assets has been the capital requirements of financial institutions. The fact that regulators have been raising and more actively policing capital requirements during the recent past has placed the spotlight on capital. A bank may have to maintain a capital ratio of 8 percent against loans on its balance sheet. So removing the loans from the balance sheet through securitization will reduce capital requirements. Furthermore, if the institution can earn the same amount of money on less capital, its return on equity will rise. Its common stock should trade at a higher price, and it is easier to raise new capital. So, the bottom line reasons to securitize assets can be powerful.

How insurance companies sometimes use ratings will serve to illustrate this point. Insurance companies invest a great deal of money in private placements. If an insurer has not made up its mind on whether to buy a security, it wants the rating agency to be very conservative and rate the prospective investment as low as possible, so it can earn a higher yield. Once it becomes an investor, however, it wants the highest rating possible in order to reduce its regulatory capital requirements. If capital requirements can be lowered, the return on the investment becomes more attractive.

The general approach of rating agencies to mortgage-backed securities is as follows. A potential issuer comes in for a preliminary conference and says, "I have $100 million in mortgages to pool, and I want to issue securities with a triple-A rating." What are our thought processes? Basically, the issuer can structure its financing to get any rating it wants. A broad body of historical data exists on the frequency of mortgage defaults and foreclosures and the severity or size of losses. There is also reliable information on how much money investors are likely to recover after foreclosure takes place. Questions such as how many loans will default, when, and how large losses will be on the individual loans can be determined for the pool. The rating agency will analyze and summarize the characteristics of the loans in the pool being evaluated and compare it to its historical data bank.

Among the underwriting characteristics perhaps most important is the loan-to-value ratio of the individual loans. Ninety percent loan-to-value ratios are significantly more risky than 50 percent loan-to-value ratios. The 50 percent loan holds a lot more equity, and the likelihood of recovering funds, even in catastrophic circumstances, is much greater.

Seasoning is also very important. Generally, if mortgages are going to go into default, it is most likely to occur during the first four years. Thus, a pool of existing home loans with an average life of four years or more would be so far along the default curve that the rating agency could justifiably require a lower level of credit enhancement on that pool or assign it a higher rating.

Geographic diversification is another consideration in rating a pool of loans. Fitch places special emphasis on this underwriting element. We have taken the country and divided it into forty-three different economic regions. We risk rate each area based on characteristics like employment levels, personal income, housing starts, home prices, and various other indices of economic activity. Our goal is to ascertain where the community may be in its regional economic cycle. Because home loan defaults seem to peak two to four years after origination, insights into what regional economic conditions will be two to four years out become important intelligence for a rating agency.

Also important to the rating of a pool is the quality of the originator of the underlying loans. What spectrum of the home mortgage market does it serve? Are its customers A, B, or C borrowers? What underwriting methods and standards does it use? What is their history as a servicer, and how do they manage delinquent loans? How quickly do local laws permit foreclosure to take place, and how effective is the servicer in realizing maximum value on distressed properties?

The rating agency will take its findings on the subject pool to its risk model to come up with an expected loss rate under normal conditions. Then we magnify the losses by assuming the catastrophic conditions of a depression. This is sometimes termed a "stress test" or "worst case analysis." Most rating agencies use the actual experience during the Great Depression of the 1930s as a worst case. At Fitch, we prefer to use the experience in Texas during the 1980s when oil prices crashed and home prices dropped by as much as 55 percent. It is a more stringent and more appropriate stress test in today's world. During the Great Depression, people typically borrowed 60 percent of the purchase price so loan-to-value ratios were approximately 60 percent. In Texas, these ratios often were 90 percent. In Texas, loans with 60 percent loan-to-value ratios defaulted in 2 or 3 cases out of 100, while over 25 out of 100 90 percent loan-to-value ratio loans went into default. And, all the 100 percent loan-to-value loans went bad. For this and other reasons, the lessons learned in Texas are much more appropriate. Regional depressions are also much more likely to be the pattern of the future.

Coming to our bottom line, assume an issuer brings in a pool and we can determine, based on our analysis, that in the absolutely worst case scenario you are going to lose 10 percent of the value of the pool. If the issuer will add credit enhancement with an assured value of 10 percent to the structure, we will rate the security triple-A. The enhancement must be designed to assure that the investor will not suffer one dollar of loss until others have absorbed the first 10 percent of loss on the pool.

On a $100 million security issue, the $10 million of credit protection can be provided in a number of ways, depending on the characteristics of the pools and the cost of the various enhancement options to the issuer. The most commonly used form of credit enhancement is the senior-subordinated structure. The issuer will place $100 million in mortgages into a trust and issue $90 million worth of senior securities and $10 million of first-loss subordinated securities. The overcollateralized senior piece is protected, for the entire pool can experience $10 million of losses without a dollar of loss to the triple-A rated senior security. The subordinated security can be sold to an investor willing to take higher risks for a greater yield or retained by the issuer. With multiclass mortgage securities, a series of securities classes can be created with differing priorities to cash flows and sequentially different ratings. Investors buying the highest risk unrated tranche know that they will not be getting back their share of the full $10 million because there will be losses. So their task is to predict how large a loss is likely and offer a price consistent with that analysis.

Another form of credit enhancement is a guarantee from a monoline insurance company. Monolines are surety companies that dedicate their entire capital to guarantee against losses on investment-grade credit risks. Because of the limits on their exposure and the dedicated capital base, they are generally rated triple-A, and the securities issues they insure can carry similar top-rank ratings. Monoline guarantees are employed in the municipal bond field and for residential mortgage-backed and asset-backed securities. Issuers offering enhanced securities with top credit ratings can benefit from having to pay the market lower interest rates on their risky assets. When the premium paid for the monoline guarantee policy is less than the interest saving achieved, it makes sense for the issuer to add the insurance feature to its offering. In rating an issue with an insurance guarantee, the rating agency must rely heavily on the quality of the monoline company. Once again, a worst case stress test is employed and applied to the insurance company. The insurance company itself becomes the weakest link in protecting the investor from loss of timely payment of interest and principal according to the terms of the contract.

The spread account is an enhancement device that is widely employed in securitizing pools of credit card loans. The easiest way to explain its use is through an example. Suppose Citibank wishes to securitize its credit card receivables. Assume cardholders are paying 21 percent on their loan balances. Citibank will have to meet 8 percent in interest and financing costs, 5 percent in losses, 2 percent in servicing costs, and 1 percent in securitization transaction costs. This comes to 16 percent and leaves a 5 percent net spread left over. This excess cash flow can be placed with the trustee and be used as a credit enhancement to protect investors against above average losses on the pool. If losses are less than the cash in the spread account, the excess funds are returned to Citibank, the issuer. To protect against unexpected losses, the rating agency is likely to ask for additional enhancements beyond the spread account.

When credit card receivables are financed as revolving credit contracts, the rating challenge becomes more complex. In this transaction, the trust takes the principal repayments received and uses them to buy more receivables from the bank. So the outstanding balances remain constant, unlike pools of residential mortgages, auto loans, or instalment loans. To protect investors and attain a higher rating, the issuer is required to agree that in the event losses hit a certain level, it will begin to amortize the outstanding pool balances. The revolver must stop revolving, and all collections from cardholders must be used to pay down the rated securities. The particular events or points at which this is to be done are called "triggers." Note that triggers enable a rating agency to rate a security higher than otherwise would be the case.

Commercial banks can provide two types of credit enhancements. One is a cash collateral loan. A bank will make a loan to the trust to absorb losses, which would enable the rating agency to upgrade its rating of the issue. The bank loan is regarded as cash collateral. As the cash flow in the cash collateral account grows and exceeds the total required by the rating agency, any excess will be used to pay back the cash collateral lender. So, the bank is making a loan to a cash collateral account and can expect to be repaid out of the spread. If the spread falls short, the bank will suffer losses on its loan. A letter of credit is another form of bank participation in the securitization process. It is first-loss protection that substitutes the credit of the bank for that of the collateral. Using the weakest link theory, rating agencies hold the view that a securities rating can be no higher than the rating of the bank providing the letter of credit. Since only one American bank, Morgan Guaranty, is rated triple-A and few foreign banks hold such a rating, the use of letters of credit is not very common today.

Legal structure and the protection accorded investors in securitized trust against bankruptcy and other types of creditor actions is another key element in securitized transactions. Rating agencies require legal opinions that the securitized assets represent a true sale and are outside the estate of the originator in the event the originator went bankrupt. Suppose a company came to Fitch and said, "I am going to issue $100 million in bonds and secure it with Treasury securities having a market value of no less than $300 million, and I agree, if the values decline, to add more Treasuries to the collateral pool. My company is a double-B credit, but I want a top rating on this pool." Fitch will not assign a triple-A rating. We would say triple-B, maybe, even though your offering is secured by the best collateral in the world. Why? The legal structure does not insulate investors from the corporate risk. Under the bankruptcy code, upon the filing of a bankruptcy petition an automatic stay prohibits any creditor from moving to take the debtors' collateral. So, although from a legal point of view the holders of the $100 million of bonds ought ultimately to get paid 100 cents on the dollar, this payment may well be delayed.

A rating is a statement that payment will be made in accordance with the terms of an obligation. That means on time. A payment default on a triple-A rated bond is front page news. The fact that investors get paid fully at some later time makes page 11. Timeliness is an element rating agencies are obsessive about.

Take a second case: If an originator sells $100 million in mortgages that have a 1 percent historic default ratio, and then it guarantees the first $10 million of losses, from the practical point of view the originator has kept all the risk. The legal question is has it or has it not sold the securities? Has the property left the estate? This question is one on which you cannot get a legal opinion. Bank regulators are of the view that an institution that retains the first loss position on a security will have to consider the entire $100 million as its risk and hold legal capital consistent with that risk. By the same token, if you sell $100 million of assets and another bank provides a $10 million letter of credit or cash collateral covering first losses, the second bank has to put up capital of only 8 percent against a base of $10 million (although both these approaches are currently under review by the banking regulators). The difference is huge.

Looking to the future, we note that the strongest driver of securitization has been the need for banks and other financial institutions to meet today's more rigorous capital requirements. As regulators adjust the capital rules on financial institutions that hold and invest the nation's savings, they will influence the volume and character of the securitization process. If a bank can remove $100 million of assets from its balance sheet, and free up, or be required to hold $8 million less of capital, value can be created. If triple-A securities pieces are accorded low capital requirements, banks will become buyers of such pieces. The challenge for the investment bankers and the capital markets is to find investors for the B, C, and unrated pieces of securitized asset pools.

Activity in Washington can also affect securitization. Congress and the administration are discussing expanding the securitization concept to additional types of assets. Bills now before Congress would enhance the securitization of commercial properties, promote the securitization of small business loans, and encourage affordable home lending. Some in Congress believe that more efficient access to capital markets via securitization can lower funding costs of meeting a broad range of social and economic goals. The Secondary Mortgage Market Enhancement Act of 1986 certainly did that for home buyers and made housing more affordable. Our government believes that market efficiencies associated with securitization create savings that can and will be passed on to the consumer. Because rated securities are liquid and easier to sell, that translates into lower yield requirements on the part of investors and lower interest costs to home buyers and other consumers.

What could happen in the marketplace to contract securitization? There are two potential risks: First, bank and other financial regulators could act, primarily through capital rules, to restrict the creation of and investment in securitized instruments. I have already commented on this potential risk. I do not believe regulators are headed in this direction. In fact, they are considering proposals in the opposite direction. Second, there is the possibility of a series of deals that go bad and expose investors to large losses. To date, there have been few bad deals, to my knowledge three—Tower Financial, Days Inn, and EPIC. They were all atypical in structure.

Tower Financial securitized health care receivables that were rated triple-A by one rating agency. The losses incurred stemmed from fraud. Receivables in the health care field are not really receivables. They are claims. The receivable is presented to an insurance company or Medicare or Medicaid, and it decides whether or not to pay it. Tower presented to the market as good receivables claims that already had been partially denied. In addition, even though the trustee was monitoring a so-called lock box, which received all payments, no one realized that some of the payments going into the lock box were actually being placed there by Tower, using funds from other parts of its operations. The trustee control systems in operation did not identify the sources of the cash. Had such a system been in place, the trustee would have realized that the outstanding receivables were not being paid off, and that the shortfall was being met from elsewhere. The lesson here is that the quality of the servicer of the loans must be evaluated carefully. A check of Tower's prior record and personnel, in my view, might have revealed the potential dangers in this case.

Days Inn securitized franchise receivables. It would sell its trade mark to hotel operators across the nation and in return receive the right to earn franchise fees for services provided. It securitized these franchise fees but received a below-investment-grade rating. Franchise fees as cash flows are different from the cash flows received from auto loans, credit cards, or home loans. In those cases, the product has been delivered, and the borrower is obligated to make payments no matter what the originator or bank may do. The franchiser has to perform in order for the franchisee to be obligated to make payments. It is an executory contract. The legal risk was, if Days Inn, which was rated B+, went into bankruptcy, under the bankruptcy code it could reject all the franchise contracts. If you have an executory contract, under the bankruptcy code, you can say, "I do not wish to meet my commitment. Find your services elsewhere." The Days Inn mark and existing receivables were transferred to and pledged by a special purpose entity. With the crown jewel, the company's mark, encumbered, management was pushed into filing the special purpose entity in bankruptcy. Actually, this was not a true securitization. The correct rating was a notch above the corporate rating itself. In a true securitization, the rating would have been triple-A or double-A.

The third default failure was EPIC, an entity that financed model homes for builders through sale of tax sheltered investments to individuals. The company raised some of its funding through sale of securities. These were private placements, not publicly rated issues. However, mortgage guaranty insurers that were rated did guarantee some of the loans and loan pools underlying the securities. When several mortgage insurers refused to pay claims on losses, alleging that they had been defrauded by misrepresentations of EPIC, their refusal raised issues for the rating agencies regarding mortgage insurer guarantees. Again, these were private placements and not rated. There is not a great deal one can do with fraud.

8

The Workings of Private Mortgage Bankers and Securitization Conduits

Mark L. Korell

An understanding of the workings of the private mortgage conduits in the residential housing market can be enhanced by the definition of two terms and one concept or relationship. The terms deserving definition are *mortgage banker* and *mortgage conduit* and the relationship is the public-private nature of finance in America's housing markets.

A *mortgage banker* is a financial entity that originates residential loans directly for home buyers through its sales or production offices, or purchases such loans from other originating entities. It underwrites and processes such contracts and subsequently services them. The mortgage banker does not invest in the home loans but sells them to a third party, such as the Federal Home Loan Mortgage Corporation (Freddie Mac) or the Federal National Mortgage Association (Fannie Mae), private institutional investors, or the capital markets. Mortgage bankers derive income from origination fees, servicing fees, and the spread between the mortgage rate and the sale price of the home loans. Mortgage bankers presently originate over 50 percent of the home loans in America, double their market share ten years ago.

A private *mortgage conduit* is a financial entity created to purchase and pool home loans and ready them for sale in securities form under its own name. The pooled mortgages become the collateral for the issuance of a security to the capital markets. Typically, private mortgage conduits are affiliates of major banks, mortgage bankers, or securities firms. Residential Funding Corporation is the conduit for my firm, GMAC Mortgage. Other prominent conduits are Bear Stearns, Citimae (Citicorp), Countrywide, GE Capital Mortgage, Prudential, and Ryland. The top three players, Prudential, Residential Funding, and GE Capital Mortgage, account for 50 percent of private volume, and all are part of very large companies (see table 8.1). Private conduits tend to focus their marketing efforts on home loans that do not conform or qualify for purchase by the federally sponsored conduits, Fannie Mae and Freddie Mac. They can and do purchase both conforming and nonconforming loans. Since Fannie Mae and Freddie Mac are limited by law to the purchase of home loans of $203,150 or less in size, the private conduits tend to be most active in the market for high-dollar or jumbo loans. More recently, private conduits have begun expanding their reach to home equity loans, B and C credit borrowers, wrap loans, multifamily, and other commercial mortgage loans.

The role of government in housing finance in the United States has a long history, going back to the Great Depression. It is based on the importance of housing in our economy, to which the economic impact of construction activity on employment and the belief in the positive social impact of home ownership on society testifies. This governmental interest is manifested today on the federal level in the three giant businesses that support—some would say control—housing, Freddie Mac, Fannie Mae, and Ginnie Mae. These government-sponsored enterprises touch two out of every three home loans originated in this country. Some describe today's system as an effective public-private partnership, pointing out that all loans are privately originated and that Freddie Mac and Fannie Mae are shareholder-owned, publicly traded companies. Others hold that the power of the government sponsored enterprises (GSEs) with minimal capital requirements so dominates the terms of trade—underwriting standards, pricing, and forms of mortgage money—that it stultifies competition and innovation and is unfair to competing portfolio lenders like thrifts and banks.

Table 8.1
Top five private mortgage-backed securities issuers
1993

Rank	Volume ($ billions)[a]	Market share (%)
Prudential	27.22	27.64
GMAC/RFC	13.04	13.24
GE Capital	8.04	8.17
Ryland/Saxon	7.45	7.56
Countrywide	6.18	6.27

Note: [a]Industry Total: $98.5 billion
Source: Inside Mortgage Capital Markets.

The Place of Private Conduits

Figure 8.1 shows the volume and growth of mortgage-backed securities outstanding at the end of each year from 1980 through 1993 for the three GSE's and for private issuers. The chart confirms the tremendous growth of the mortgage-backed securities market from $100 billion in 1980 and $400 billion in 1985 to almost $1.5 trillion at the end of 1993. The GSEs dominate the market. The small sliver at the top of the chart represents the contribution of private mortgage securities. At $164 billion at year's end 1993, it accounted for 10.8 percent of outstandings. The slope of both the total line and the private conduit line indicate that growth is continuing. Although the disappearance in 1994 of home loan refinancing volume will interrupt the trend, I have every confidence that future housing demand will bring a return of growth to both private and total activity.

In terms of annual issuance, the 1993 volume for GSEs and private issuers is shown in figure 8.2. Private issuers accounted for 15 percent of new volume, an all-time high, albeit well below the GSE dominance.

The placement or distribution of private mortgage-backed securities to investors is done by national securities firms, with familiar names heading the list (see table 8.2). In 1993, Kidder Peabody, Lehman, First

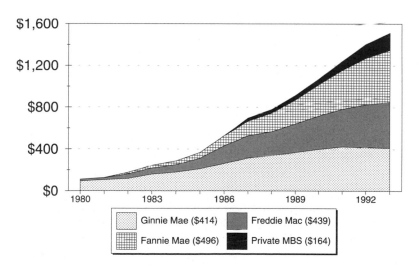

Figure 8.1
Volume of mortgage-backed securities outstanding: 1980–1993 ($ billions)
Source: Mortgage Market Statistical Annual for 1994.

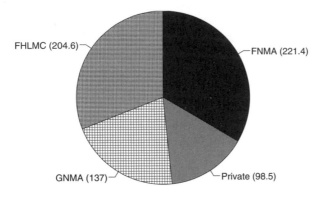

Total securities issued: $661.5 billion

Figure 8.2
GSE versus private issuance of mortgage-backed securities, 1993 ($ billions)
Source: Inside Mortgage Capital Markets.

Boston, Bear Stearns, and Salomon were the principal underwriters of private conduit offerings, distributing 56 percent of the $98.5 billion of new issues. Thus, the business exhibits a high degree of concentration both on the part of conduit sponsors and on the part of investment banking underwriters. It is a specialized business, and I believe it will get more concentrated in the years ahead as the private market becomes more sophisticated in both loan product and securitization techniques.

Consolidation: The Major Trend

The major business trend in the private conduit business today is consolidation. The major forces supporting this trend are listed in table 8.3. These forces seem to be quite powerful and may very well be a response to the fact that private companies must compete in an origination and investment market dominated by very powerful government-sponsored enterprises. Fannie Mae and Freddie Mac set the tone and terms of competition in much the same way that American Telephone and Telegraph once did in the phone business. Consolidation is coming about very quickly and is likely to continue.

Access to capital is a driving force behind this trend to fewer and larger players. The top three conduits, accounting for 49 percent of all private conduit securitization in 1993, were each subsidiaries of the largest companies in the United States—Prudential Insurance Com-

Table 8.2
Top five private mortgage-backed securities underwriters
1993

Rank	Volume ($ billions)[a]	Market share (%)
Kidder, Peabody	15.40	15.63
Lehman Brothers	12.20	12.37
First Boston	11.02	11.19
Bear, Stearns	9.09	9.23
Salomon Brothers	7.95	8.07

Note: [a]Industry Total: $98.5 Billion
Source: Inside Mortgage Capital Markets.

Table 8.3
Forces encouraging consolidation in the private conduit field

- Greater access to capital
- Better performance of large pools
  - Greater liquidity
  - Better pricing
  - Better executions
  - Greater geographic diversification
- Economies of scale
  - Origination costs
  - Fixed processing costs
- Greater access to sophisticated modeling and performance technologies
- Greater access to overseas investment markets

pany, General Motors, and General Electric. It requires a great deal of capital to make loans, buy and warehouse loans, hedge them, and then aggregate mortgages into pools big enough to get the best execution. Participants in the game have to have billions of dollars of capital at their disposal. That may come from parent companies. It may come from borrowings that require parent guarantees. The key point is that funding needs of conduits are large and have been growing. Ten years ago $50 million deals were being done. Five or six years ago, a $100 million offering was a notable deal. Today, Residential Funding routinely plans to do $500 million deals. And that is the size of transactions in the private conduit market. In the GSE market, deals get even larger.

A second reason why consolidation will continue is that larger deals provide investors with better investment products or executions, and they will pay the conduit for the values created. Why is that? Rating agencies and investors look with favor on mortgage pools that exhibit greater geographical diversification. It is desirable to have loans on properties across the nation in your pools. Because specific regional economies may produce concentrations of risk at some future date and geographic concentrations of loans can jeopardize investment perfor- mance, investors will pay more for pools with geographically diver- sified collateral. In addition, the risk models used by rating agencies like Fitch will give you positive credit for geographic dispersal. The creation of larger pools enables conduits to include more loans in each pool and increase its geographic diversification. Not all triple-A pools are the same. Investors are learning to differentiate on the basis of geography and other risk elements. Conduit managers are responding by building diversification into larger pools.

Another benefit of large pools is that conduit transactions create a number of relatively high fixed costs—legal fees, accounting fees, structuring and registration fees, and the cost of building and main- taining a quality infrastructure at the central administration and proc- essing center. A key management goal is to spread those costs over more volume. This helps to reduce unit costs and enhances net profits.

Another market force arguing for consolidation and larger deals is investor desire for greater predictability of cash flows and the ability to evaluate and price prepayment risk. Conduit managers seek to meet this need by offering mortgage product and coupon segregation in their deals. Providing this benefit requires large pools and a reliable body of historical data. We will seek, for example, to create deals with a single type of mortgage in them. So, all fifteen-year mortgages will go into one pool, all thirty-year mortgages into another pool, and so on. Each homogeneous pool will trade more predictably than if we were to mix mortgages of differing maturities in a single pool. The goal in purifying the collateral is to increase the predictability of performance of the pool and thereby respond to the investor question: "Gee, what happens if rates go up?" Eliminating uncertainty can lead to easier sales, better executions, and higher prices in both the primary and secondary market transactions.

Coupon segregation is another important investor preference. If you have all 8 percent coupon mortgages in a mortgage security, that deal will trade better and sell for more than a pool with a mix of mortgages from, say, 7 percent to 9 percent. Why? Because the prepayment rate is going to be more predictable, more even in the former deal than in the latter one. If rates go down, the 9 percent loans will pay off or refinance, and the 7 percent loans will continue in the portfolio. Investors are going to have principal funds returned in a partial manner. If you have a narrow coupon range, like the 8 percent pool, your prepayment risk becomes somewhat easier to anticipate, price, and handle.

What does the desire for mortgage product and coupon homogeneity on the part of the investor mean to the conduit manager? To meet this need and profit from it, you must have a wide range of home loan product coming into your inventory or warehouse. The loan flow must be sufficient to fill up a fifteen-year bucket or pool, a thirty-year pool, a one-year adjustable loan pool, and a LIBOR-based pool on a timely basis. Only with a large flow of multiple product originations can you create the efficient, large-size securitization issues that the market will find particularly attractive. This, again, argues for larger conduit companies.

The increase in the complexity of securitized mortgage deals, particularly the explosion in the number of classes created out of individual pools under the REMIC legislation, also favors large deals and large conduit companies. In the past conduits would rely on Wall Street to do the financial engineering on multitranche issues. They had the big computers and the "rocket scientists" to operate them. Now, some of us have reached a size where we can afford and have made the investment in software that allows us to independently model our own deals. Technology becomes an in-house asset.

Large conduits with many issues outstanding and trading in the secondary market have an advantage over small or occasional conduit issuers in terms of performance in the after market. They can offer better liquidity for their issues in the secondary market and better pricing. From a rating agency view, the more deals a conduit has in the market, the easier it is for the agency to get comfortable with an issuer, and the more comfortable investors become. This is especially helpful in overseas markets. The no-name players have a difficult time gaining acceptance overseas. An increasing share of the investor market for mortgage securities is overseas. Their comfort level with an issuer rises noticeably when they can pick up a phone and get two or three bids on a particular bond. Size, multiple issues outstanding, and name recognition are valuable assets to the conduit issuer.

Looking Ahead

Looking ahead, we can see that one of the primary challenges facing the secondary mortgage markets is the free put we have given to mortgage borrowers (see table 8.4). Individual homeowners creating a thirty-year or fifteen-year fixed-rate mortgage can prepay that mortgage before maturity without prepayment penalties or other costs. This can be done, not on a predetermined date, as with a callable bond, but at any time the borrower chooses. The time the borrower chooses, as you might expect is very likely to be the time when the investor would least like to be repaid. If you have a 10 percent loan and market rates drop to 7.5 percent, you are very likely to pay off the outstanding balance on that loan and refinance at the lower rate. Zero point loans, by cutting transaction costs, encourage such transactions. Turning rate trends around, you can see that if you got a 7.5 percent mortgage twelve months ago, with mortgage rates 8.5 percent and higher today, you are going to stay with the 7.5 percent loan and not pay it ahead of schedule at all. Investors anticipating reasonable amounts of prepayments are in for a surprise. The secondary mortgage markets react by adjusting the prices of mortgage securities. During the past six months the prices on mortgage pools containing 7.5 percent loans dropped significantly. The contract, in large part because of consumer protection attitudes in Washington and some states, notably California, is unbalanced. It favors the homeowner and penalizes the investor.

What will be done? Loans with prepayment penalties are reentering the market. Lenders will offer you a lower interest rate or start rate on a loan if you will agree to make a suitable exit payment to investors if and when you return principal ahead of schedule. The assumable

Table 8.4
Current market challenges facing private conduit managers

- Forecasting and managing prepayment risk
- Relief from homeowners free "put" (refinancing risk)
- Demand for more data on risks in underlying loans
- Changing nature of investors in securitized product
  - Mutual funds
  - International investors
  - Investors in lower-rated securities
- Developing and expanding the secondary/secondary market

loan is another technique that can slow prepayments. It simply says that the loan does not have to be paid off if you move. It can go with the property and be assumed by the next buyer if that buyer qualifies for the debt. The investor here can expect the average life of the pool to be longer because of this feature. Additional efforts will be made by creators of mortgage pools to meet investor objections to the uncertainty of principal repayment. The challenge is an artful one. Homeowners are going to resist. They know they have a good thing in the ability to refinance without penalty. Investors know they can pay more for pool investment with protection against prepayment risk built in. The issue is one of pricing the option correctly.

I should also note that high-dollar or jumbo loans tend to have a higher prepayment risk due to refinancing than middle-market loans. If interest rates decline from 8 percent to 7.5 percent, refinancing a $100,000 loan will save the home buyer about $35 per month. Refinancing a $300,000 loan will save the home buyer $105 per month. If 100 homeowners in each class look at the math, significantly more will be moved to action by the $100+ per month saving than by the $35 saving. Stated another way, jumbo loan borrowers will be moved to consider refinancing at smaller rate swings. One result of this market fact is that investors will likely demand higher spreads over noncallable Treasuries to purchase mortgage-backed securities with jumbo loans for collateral. Investors seek to be paid for uncertainty and volatility as well as for taking interest rate and credit risk.

Another challenge is the growing demand from investors for more information on the home loans within the securitized pool. This is somewhat ironic. When we first introduced investors to securitized mortgage product, the big appeal was that investors did not have to look at individual loans in detail. Loans were wrapped into a big tradable security, credit enhancers would take the first losses, and the rating agencies would bless the issue with a triple-A rating. If loans were 80 percent loan-to-value or 90 percent loan-to-value, or in Minnesota, Texas, or California, it mattered not because the enhancer would be there to cover credit losses. Why worry? Investors found that there were regional differences in losses and that these losses became increased prepayments. There was also the question of the size of the aggregate losses. So, we are being asked to dig out data on the underlying loans in individual pools. We are disclosing more and more because institutional investors demand the comfort of greater knowledge. We have come full circle, and in some ways lost one of the efficiencies of securitization. In other ways the market has become more efficient and is demanding more complete or perfect information.

Who are the buyers of private conduit paper? To this point they have mirrored buyers of GSE and other mortgage paper. Looking forward, foreign investors are becoming a great deal more knowledgeable about mortgage investment, and their share of the investment market will increase. Their interest in non-GSE, private, mortgage-backed securities is good because they like the higher yields here. They like the triple-A. They like the big names of the major players. They are attracted by the liquidity being developed in the market sector. Presently, about 10 to 20 percent of Residential Funding's issues will be sold in Europe and the Far East. That could easily double in the next five years, as investment experience with mortgage product grows. The appetite for information is tremendous.

Mutual funds are the fastest growing segment of investors in mortgage-backed securities. They are attracting billions of dollars in 401(k) funds, IRAs, and other small capital pools that can handle some mortgage and real estate risk. The REITs (Real Estate Investment Trusts) are an ideal vehicle for our higher risk tranches. Even commercial mortgage-backed securities are now being mixed into mortgage-backed securities mutual funds.

To illustrate the pace of development, let me note the emergence of what I will call, for want of a better name, the secondary/secondary market in mortgage securities. The primary market is mortgage origination. The secondary market is mortgage sales to investors in securitized form by conduits like Residential Funding. The secondary/secondary market is the retrading, the recombination into new securities issues of product that is already trading in the secondary market. The deal may take a tranche from a Prudential mortgage security, another tranche from an RFC issue, and a Freddie Mac piece and put them together on the basis of computer modeling to create a brand-new security with properties currently attractive to the investor market. With a total of $1.5 trillion mortgage debt outstanding, the development of a secondary/secondary market does seem just a matter of time. The sophistication of the investment banking and trading elements of the market continues to grow. As investor understanding and appetite for risk grows concomitantly, a whole new stage of development will appear. Major players will see their role grow from a new direction.

Summing Up

The residential mortgage markets will continue to grow. Baby boomers will trade up and have the resources to purchase more expensive homes. Credit performance has been good. The exposure caused by overly aggressive financial engineering will subside as understanding of the new instruments and the risks implicit in them increases. We will see losses on the lower rated bonds. Statistically, it should happen. When it happens, there will be lawsuits and calls for regulatory and legislative protection. The preferred results of such losses in free and competitive markets should be to learn from one's mistakes and to invest in greater due diligence, more skillful collection and analysis of information on risk. The necessary learning curve as these still young markets evolve will again favor the larger, better capitalized players in the private conduit field.

We can also expect private conduits to seek new growth by increasingly expanding their reach to meeting shelter needs outside the traditional one-to-four-family house and to new product lines. Mobile home loans, home equity loans, second mortgages, and various types of commercial property loans will be among the target markets. Wherever a critical mass of loan volume can be captured, private conduits can be expected to try to apply their securitization talents to reducing funding costs and earning a profit.

The mortgage securities market is highly dynamic. Changes in the direction of interest rates and the slope of the Treasury yield curve can occur quickly and lead to major changes in mortgage volume and the type of securitized loan product desired by investors. Financial regulators and the Financial Accounting Standards Board (FASB) can propose or enact changes that will materially affect investment preferences and yields. Capital requirements and mark-to-market rules have a special power to affect mortgage markets. The dynamism in this market makes the private conduit business attractive. Change for us equals opportunity. Private conduits may well be able to adjust to market forces more quickly than the federal conduits. In a market that wants, not just vanilla, chocolate and strawberry, but at least thirty-three flavors, market-driven private players who are entrepreneurial and agile should be successful.

9

Securitization from the Investor View: Meeting Investor Needs with Products and Price

Neil Kochen

Securitized assets are an important and growing part of the investment portfolios of many life insurance companies and other institutional investors. To understand how a particular type of investor would use securitized products, one is advised to have in mind the liability structure of the organization, as well as its investment philosophy. Balance sheet and liquidity needs and risk preferences can drive investment choices. When a new family of investment products reaches market, the learning curve tends to be steep—albeit uneven from firm to firm. With securitized products, we are still early on that learning curve for many investors. This makes the field both more interesting and more risky than it may be later. I am concerned particularly about some of the marketing illusions that have grown up around securitized product. The illusions of liquidity, the illusion of the triple-A rating, as well as the illusion of yield should be addressed.

Aetna as an Institutional Investor

First, a brief overview of Aetna Life and Casualty is in order. Aetna is the fourth largest U.S. insurer. As of the end of 1993, it had $98 billion of assets under management to fund its four primary lines of business. In the medical insurance and health business, the investment department manages funds to support insurance operations, as well as assets of HMOs (health maintenance organizations), which must meet the costs of long-term care. The indemnity insurance business is a second area of operation, and one where investment managers must be sensitive to different liability patterns. This includes auto and homeowners risk, as well as a large block of commercial casualty business for corporations and workmen's compensation coverage. The third business area is the traditional life insurance business—individual life, whole life, term life, universal life, and group life. Finally, one of our largest responsibilities is meeting the investment needs of our asset-accumulation businesses. Here, we are investing funds for private and public defined contribution and defined benefit pension plans, 401(k) plans, other types of pooled investment funds, and individual annuity funds. Our presence in international markets is growing. Aetna has offices in Canada, Mexico, Chile, England, and the Far East.

Table 9.1 shows the general accounts of Aetna's operating insurance companies. The differences in the investment portfolios reflect the differences in the funding needs of the various lines of business. Note that securitized products fit most readily into Aetna Life Insurance and Annuity Corporation (ALIAC), the accounts managed for individuals and small pension funds. In our view, both the Life Insurance Company and the Property and Casualty Company are overweighted in the commercial mortgage loan market. We currently have over 40 percent of the assets of the Life Company and 16 percent of the assets of the Property and Casualty Company in this investment class. In years past, the investment strategy was basically buy and hold. We did not fully value the changing risk elements in those markets during the 1980s. Since 1989, we have been making significant efforts to reduce our exposure to this very difficult market and have done so. New funds in these portfolios are being invested in public bonds. There has also been growth in the size of holdings of securitized assets in these portfolios.

The nature of the liabilities facing the Aetna Life Insurance and Annuity Corporation enables it to be tolerant of the prepayment risks and other exposures inherent in mortgage-backed securities and CMOs (collateralized mortgage obligations). Thus, its investment portfolio can include a high percentage of such products and enjoy the higher yields offered. As of year's end 1993, 59 percent of ALIAC's assets were invested in securitized products, although since that time, our holdings of securitized assets, primarily CMOs, has fallen dramatically.

Aetna's investment philosophy can best be described as a total return focus. Bond portfolios are marked to market regularly, some weekly and some monthly, depending on the nature of the corresponding liabilities. We compute total return and compare our performance to such publicly available benchmarks as Treasury indices, the Shearson-Lehman Index, and others. Close attention is paid to matching liquidity of invested assets to liability needs of operating units. We match duration very closely and seek to limit prepayment, yield curve, or liquidity risk. Employing an 80/20 rule, we focus 80 percent of our

Table 9.1
General accounts of Aetna Life & Casualty
(December 31, 1993)

Assets	Aetna Life Insurance Co. ($ billions)	Property and Casualty Group ($ billions)	Aetna Life Insurance and Annuity Corp. ($ billions)
Bonds	16.4	11.3	9.9
Mortgage loans	13.3	2.2	0.0
Real estate	1.2	0.2	0.0
Common/equity	0.4	0.6	0.2
Cash/short-term	0.4	0.2	0.5
Other	0.5	0.6	0.0
Total	32.3	15.1	10.6
Bonds			
Treasury/agency	3.6	3.4	0.8
Corporate	8.4	5.3	2.0
Foreign	2.0	0.7	0.8
Securitized	2.4	1.9	6.3
Total	16.4	11.3	9.9

time on the 20 percent of assets that, by virtue of their risk, require more active management attention. The categories requiring special investment attention would include problem mortgage loans, below-investment-grade bonds, higher risk mortgage-backed securities and CMOs, and foreign exposure in emerging markets. A good deal of time is spent in discussions with our internal business clients and external clients to ensure that the risk profile of the underlying portfolios are in keeping with their needs and desires.

Aetna and many other insurance companies during the 1980s invested 75 to 80 percent of their funds in private placements and commercial mortgage loans. The result of this investment strategy was to load up the credit risk basket to the brim, albeit with different types of credit risk. Under our current total return philosophy, we are looking to incorporate some interest rate risk, repayment risk, and foreign currency risk in portfolios as a way to diversify away from credit risk.

The Place of Securitized Assets in Portfolios

A primary objective of a major institution investing in securitized assets is to further the risk diversification within its bond portfolio, as well as to improve diversification of its mortgage portfolio. The opportunity to enhance total return through opportunistic analysis and investment in the growing array of securitized products flowing from a creative Wall Street adds further attraction to the investment field. The high credit quality designed into these securitized products allows us to diversify without increasing credit risk in the overall portfolio. Maintaining a high credit-quality portfolio is attractive for rating agency purposes and has appeal to institutional investors and other external clients. Finally, the liquidity of securitized holdings has been better than the liquidity of some other fixed-income products, such as private placements. This makes that all important liability-asset match easier to accomplish.

At Aetna, we divide the securitized-asset market into three broad categories. For want of better terms, we call them the stable securitized market, the evolving securitized market, and the experimental securitized market, one that is still in its infancy.

The stable market is essentially populated by pass-through investment products—mortgage-backed securities, CARDs (Certificates for Amortizing Revolving Debts), CARs (Certificates for Automobile Receivables), lease receivables, and so on. The characteristics of the sector are listed in table 9.2. The legal and investment structures are well established and understood by the market place. There is broad agreement on the analytics used to assess expected return and risk. The base of historical experience on these investments is growing and has been tested over an economic downturn and interest-rate cycle. The measures to be used in evaluating performance are becoming standardized, and given these positive developments, the universe of investors active in the market is growing. The stable securitized products are demonstrating a significantly lower volatility than other securitized assets and as a consequence are lowering total return opportunities. That is why the label "stable markets" applies. To the degree that any securi-

Table 9.2
Stable markets

Mortgage-backed securities, cars, lease receivables

• Structures established and well understood

• Broad agreement on analytics

• History

• Lower volatility, total return opportunities

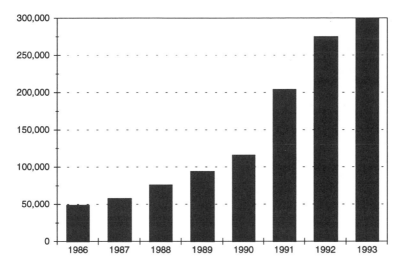

Figure 9.1
Agency CMO issuance: GNMA, FHLMC, and FNMA ($ millions)
Source: First Boston.

tized market might be considered a routine investment vehicle, this category is one. Aetna will invest in this market in a different manner than in the more complex and volatile CMO market. Currently, our combined portfolios hold about $4 billion in mortgage-backed securities and between $500 million and $600 million in CARs and CARDs and some marine or boat loan receivables.

The second major category of investment holdings is collateralized mortgage securities. In terms of new issuance, this has been the major growth sector in securitized markets over the past seven or eight years. Figure 9.1 shows federal agency issuance since 1986. Private conduit offerings have been growing as well. The way Wall Street uses the term CMOs and calls mortgage-backed securities "collateral"—as if they were not a security in their own right rather than building blocks for the CMO market—can be taken as evidence of the acceptance of these concepts and products in investment markets. Nevertheless, investors should not forget that this market is still evolving with regard to structures and history. How it will react under stress has yet to be determined. That is why Aetna classes CMO securities as an evolving market.

The commercial mortgage-backed securities market was slow in starting because of the difficulties in bringing together the elements necessary for efficient conversion of debt into securities and the troubled nature of the commercial property market in terms of value. The efforts of the Resolution Trust Corporation (RTC) to sell distressed real estate it owned via securitization with very heavy overcollateralization several years ago created a flurry of activity. It also established a pattern that others—banks and insurance companies with real estate owned, for example—could follow in unloading mortgage loans and properties on their books. However, we view the markets here as in their infancy, even experimental, and feel that there is a long way to go before markets reach agreement as to the standardized structure and the necessary sense of history on these securities.

The Evolution of CMO Markets

Table 9.3 shows the continuing evolution of the CMO deals by contrasting the features in the early deals to those that one might find in current offerings. The plain vanilla structure of early CMOs was marked by simple four- to eight-tranche structures with well-understood prioritizations. Aetna was a significant participant in the PAC (planned amortization class) market. These were sold to us as corporate bond substitutes, and we were attracted by their defined amortization schedule and significant protection against prepayment risk. Looking back at these early contracts, we are finding greater than expected decay in duration and poorer performance in the total return of these bonds. Leverage and model risk (a term I will describe later) were low.

Table 9.3
Evolution of collateralized mortgage obligation markets

Early deals	Current trends
Plain vanilla collateral	Complex collateral
Simple structures (4–8 tranches)	Complex structures (90+ tranches)
Well-understood prioritization	Uncertain prioritizations
PACs: Strong call protection (wide bands)	Proliferation of PAC-like structures (TACs, VADMs, PAC II, PAC IO)
Low leverage on prepayments	High embedded leverage
Low "model risk"	High "model risk"

The recent issues offered in the market have significantly more complex structures. In some cases we are seeing the original CMO tranches being tranched again (called "Re-REMICS"). This makes the analysis of the nature of the underlying collateral and prospective performance of the new CMO tranche very difficult. One Freddie Mac REMIC brought to my attention recently had over ninety tranches in it—that is ninety different securities with differing features. I do not believe that investment managers can fully understand the risk characteristics of any single tranche in a deal of that complexity. The tools we have on the investment side to analyze the riskiness of such issues has lagged far behind the capacity of the people in Wall Street to manufacture these synthetic securities.

The strong desire of investors for call protection and avoidance of prepayment risk has prompted the creation of CMOs with a higher number of TAC (targeted amortization class), VADM (very accurately defined maturity), PAC II, and PAC IO (interest only) tranches. Although such securities have more protection than support bonds or sequentials or other securities, they certainly have significantly less call protection than the early, less complex mortgage securities.

A growing number of the CMO issues have embedded in their complex tranche structure much higher degrees of leverage. If prepayments deviate from the planned levels, even slightly, one can see securities that virtually fall off the table in terms of price and performance. This is in marked contrast to the risk profile of early CMO structures. When prepayments fell outside the expected or planned band, there might well be a diminution in value, but not a falling-off-the-table performance because of leverage.

"Model risk" refers to the ability of an investor to forecast with quantitative tools the expected performance or rates of return on an investment in a particular collateralized mortgage security tranche. The complexity of the issues and the stress that complexity put on the assumptions implicit in the model heightened measurably the risk of faulty analysis.

A review of the fast-paced development of the CMO market during its first ten years is shown in figure 9.2. Wall Street responded to investor demands in a very rapid fashion. In the early 1980s an investor had a choice of three or four flavors. By 1989, you could almost name your flavor. If it did not exist, some dealer would create it as part of his firm's next securitization. And, I would suggest, we are not done yet with the slicing and dicing that has become a Wall Street art

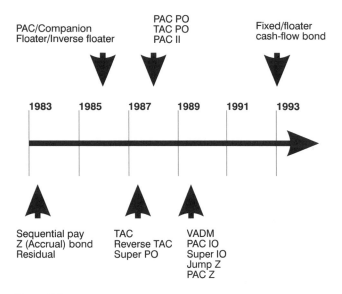

Figure 9.2
The development of the CMO market
Source: Salomon Brothers.

form. As investors reach for yield, as they seek to find outlets for funds that formerly flowed directly into real estate, as funds flows are redirected from the high-yield corporate securities field, there is a natural tendency to move out the risk spectrum in areas that are producing new offerings. To accommodate this demand Wall Street will produce structures that promise the desired yields. Recognizing that our capital markets are fairly efficient, I remind you there are no free lunches. You do not get high yields without the accompanying risk. CMO and derivative investors will learn that lesson.

Experience with the CMO market in residential mortgages can be instructive for the development of the commercial mortgage securities market. This latter market is evolving in a very similar manner. The early deals, dated from around 1992, involved very simple structures—typically two or three tranches for the landmark RTC deals. The collateral was well diversified geographically and by property type, as well as by size. Most of the deals were large and tended to homogenize a good deal of the risk involved in the individual commercial mortgages. Strong credit protection was dictated for the senior tranches through overcollateralization. For example, in RTC's first deal, 1992-C1, you would have to suffer a 50 percent loss of cash flow, absorbed first by the cash collateral account and then by the subordinated tranches, before the senior tranche experienced a cash shortfall. Currently the collateral protection for senior tranches is significantly less and the spreads over Treasuries have narrowed. In a pattern similar to the one that occurred in the residential field, there is growing evidence that the market acceptance of commercial mortgage securitization is increasing. As experience grows, the market can be expected to move toward more complex structures, weaker collateral, tighter pricing spreads to Treasuries, and reduced credit protection.

The Illusions in Securitized Markets

Working in securitized capital markets leaves one with the impression that key features of these markets are being oversold. The promise offered to investors may be running ahead of the ultimate historic reality. I call these illusions, and there are three of particular concern—the illusion of liquidity, the illusion of triple-A rating, and the illusion of high yield. The CMO market raises the greatest concerns, but the illusions are present to a degree in the commercial mortgage-backed market and among CARs, CARDs, and lease receivables as well.

Turning to liquidity, we may find it instructive first to review how differently Wall Street structures residential CMOs and commercial mortgage-backed securities. In the CMO market, investment bankers take homogeneous collateral, bundles of home loans, and through securitization create heterogeneous securities. A major objective of the process is to allocate prepayment risk among investors with different appetites for risk. By way of contrast, in the commercial mortgage-backed market, investment bankers take very heterogeneous collateral and through securitization create homogeneous securities. The objective here once again is to allocate credit risk in the manner desired by investors with different risk appetites.

Deal structure has a material affect on liquidity. Knowledge of the structure of the deal and the nature of the underlying collateral are critical to assessing the liquidity of one's investment holdings. The amount of leverage in a tranche—the degree to which it will respond to small movements in interest rates, for example—can affect marketability and price. Consider the hedge fund Granite Partners and its manager, David Askin. This firm specialized in trading highly leveraged CMOs and derivatives, and when interest rates moved against them, margin calls were made. To meet margin calls, Granite became a very aggressive seller and the Street was more than happy to bid its collateral down ten, twenty and sometimes thirty basis points to what it felt was fair value, given the fact that there were few other bids. Granite did not survive the margin calls.

The lesson here is that in volatile-interest-rate environments, the heterogeneous types of securities found in the CMO market can suffer from a lack of liquidity. Homogeneous, commodity-type investments are the most liquid. Following my logic, we should then find it true that the commercial mortgage-backed securities will be more liquid than the underlying collateral, the properties. However, the test of time has not yet validated that conclusion. One thing we do know at Aetna: In volatile environments, commodity-type investments are the most liquid. As a guide to market discipline, we like the expression, "Sure they're liquid, unless you actually have to sell them!"

The second illusion is the triple-A illusion. Credit-rating agencies will tell you their ratings address the likelihood of timely payment of interest and ultimate return of principal. The rating does not address the timing of the return of principal. Their income analysis focuses on a static yield as well. The combination of those factors tends to paint a picture of a triple-A security as one having a very dependable, timely return and a minimal risk on the asset side. The course of interest rates over the past few years provided an interesting real-time test of these premises for securitized assets. The dramatic decline of interest rates since 1991, followed by the sharp reversal of rates during 1994, has shown that prepayment risk is significantly more onerous than credit risk.

An investor purchasing a mortgage-backed security or CMO tranche with a triple-A rating may be lulled into a false sense of complacency. The economic risk (as contrasted to the legal risk) in the holding can be substantially greater than the triple-A rating implies. One question for an investor is, would you rather have a bond default and receive 80 cents on the dollar on a timely basis or get an early prepayment and receive 100 cents on the dollar? From an accounting perspective, the prepayment is better because you will show no loss. You lent $100 and received $100 back. From an economic perspective, the outcome to be preferred depends very much on the interest-rate environment. If you hold an 8 percent, ten-year bond and interest rates are at a 12 percent level and you get 80 cents on the dollar via a default, you may well make money by reinvesting the funds received at the now higher interest-rate level. Alternatively, if you have an 8 percent, ten-year bond with call exposure, and rates decline by fifty basis points, pre-payments can occur, and you will suffer an economic loss on reinvest-ment. Instead of having a security that experienced a market gain in a falling rate environment, you now get back par and face a reinvest-ment challenge. So, the triple-A rating, which says there is no risk at default, becomes illusionary. Investors should not be misled and be-lieve that they will not be confronted by a measure of default risk.

As a manager of commercial properties, Aetna finds from time to time that even though a deal is noncallable, it frequently will take early prepayments at par, or even at a discount. We do this because it is more prudent than honoring the legal documentation and running the risk of getting back only forty cents or fifty cents on the dollar at a later date. This is good property management. Within a trust structure there should be potential for the better manager to take some early prepayments as sound practice. The effect of this action, with a shifting infrastructure, is going to fall much harder on the senior triple-A tranches than the junior tranches.

Next, I want to comment on the yield illusion. Investment markets have come to recognize that high yield does not necessarily equal high return. In years past, real estate investing at a given duration was essentially a yield game. Investors knew that they could not compare the yield on a two-year security with an eight-year security. Yet, within the realm of eight-year securities, one could look for the highest yield for a given level of risk. Real estate investing was a yield game. Today, real estate investing has turned into an option-adjusted spread game. Market participants say, "Here is a five-year-duration CMO or mort-gage-backed pass-through, and it has an option adjusted spread of X." The option adjusted spread calculation is a way to value the imbedded prepayment option. You work out the value of an option, and that is then the expected return.

The problem with this investment logic is that not all securities at the same option-adjusted spread, even at the same duration, have the same risk characteristics. They can have different leverage ratios, vola-tility, prepayment risk, and model risk, despite identical spread char-acteristics. For example, there are interest-only strips (IOs), which have been branded as a type of toxic waste by the market and priced way off any curve. In the CMO market some special tranches can trade at option-adjusted spreads twelve hundred basis points off the Treasury curve because investors still feel they are not being compensated for the prepayment or structure risk imbedded within these securities.

It is Aetna's view that the prudent investor must model total expected return. We incorporate in our analysis of a security not only an expected yield but also the potential total return over a series of likely scenarios across a range of interest-rate environments. Our goal is to uncover the underlying interest rate and model risk imbedded in these complex, multifaceted securities. We do this by modeling the dynamic underlying fundamentals, including interest rates, credit defaults, spread risk, and model risk across a number of scenarios.

Finally, let me focus on model risk. In order to evaluate a mortgage-backed security or a CMO, the analyst must make an assumption on the likelihood of prepayment in different interest-rate environments. During the last couple of years we have witnessed an exogenous shift in the reaction of home borrowers to changes in the level of interest rates. They have become much more efficient in the exercise of their prepayment rights, primarily due to changes in the mortgage-lending industry. Since mortgage bankers are primarily in the loan-servicing business as opposed to the portfolio investment game, which occupied the savings and loans, it is now worth their while to aggressively market refinancings to individual home owners. They do this to retain the servicing income on the underlying mortgage. The alternative is to see the home borrower prepay and move the servicing to a competing institution. This business objective plus the heightened price competition in the home mortgage field that spawned zero point refinancing have increased borrower response rates to interest-rate changes. Such competition has certainly been in the best interest of the home owner, and perhaps in the best interest of the individual mortgage banker/servicer. The problem is the investor takes it on the chin. These dramatic shifts in the retail market for home loans have produced a large shift in the statistical curve that we use to estimate the sensitivity of homeowners to interest-rate shifts. They have rendered the underlying mortgage-backed securities in the portfolios of investors significantly more risky than our models would have suggested one or two years ago. This is a prime example of model risk, and new tests must be developed to evaluate it.

Our analysts perform a tremendous amount of statistical analysis on investments in securities assets. Even so, the models go wrong. They are statistical estimations. For some issues, the estimates of prepayment speeds may approximate the forecasts. But for others the estimates can be significantly different from actual outcomes. For example, take a FNMA 9 percent, mortgage-backed security in today's market. We shocked the prepayment curve up and down by 20 percent to reflect the changing borrower prepayment patterns and found that the option adjusted spread varied by ten to twelve basis points. The standard mortgage security is not highly sensitive to the shift in the prepayment curve. However, when testing several IOs and POs, which have significantly more built-in leverage, we found the same 20 percent up-and-down test produced a move in the option-adjusted spread and expected return of plus and minus two hundred basis points. In one case there was a spread of twelve hundred basis points. That is a product of leverage and illustrates the measure of model risk extant in investing in securitized product.

Management Guidelines for Securitized Products

Aetna and most other institutional investors purchase and manage not only CMO type securities but a broad range of asset-backed securities. From a portfolio management perspective, it is important to establish an overall investment strategy and to persist with that strategy (see table 9.4).Obviously, one must carefully analyze each security at purchase. However, it is even more important to continually monitor one's holdings. Interest rates can move dramatically. Underlying credit fundamentals can change fairly quickly in a regional market. The risk profile of securities, especially those that have built-in leverage like CMOs, is inherently volatile and demands close and continuous monitoring. In one month you may find you have the desired match of a 3-year duration in your portfolio assets and the liabilities you are

Table 9.4
Guidelines for managing securitized products

- Establish investment strategy and persist
- Carefully analyze at purchase
- Continually monitor holdings (high cost)
- Understand dynamic aspects of deal structure
- Do not succumb to apparent free lunch
- Understand total return
- Analyze all aspects of risk—credit, prepayment, liquidity, model, etc.
- Determine suitability for liabilities
- Invest in technology
- Do not be lulled into false sense of security
- Remember purchase decisions are easier to make than sell decisions

funding. At the next quarterly review, because of a significant increase in market rates, you can find the duration of your assets dropped one or two years. You have a serious mismatch that can have an impact on policyholders' surplus or shareholders' rates of return.

Yield can be very enticing, even alluring. My counsel is do not succumb to the apparent free lunch. There is a great deal more to total return than just current yield. At the day's end, it is total return that puts money in your pocket and pays the bills. Take time to understand the illusions of liquidity, triple-A ratings, and high yield.

In summary, although I pointed out the cautions and illusions that must be recognized by investors in the securitized debt market, I hasten to point out that Aetna is a large user of this growing and rapidly evolving outlet for funds. We believe there is a great deal of value in this market. Those investors who have critical mass and can invest in technology and talent should find this market to their liking. There is significant money to be made, albeit at a slightly higher risk profile, even in the lower risk components of this market. Remember to develop a good command of total return. To focus simply on yield will do nothing but get you in trouble, and do not stop at an option-adjusted spread analysis. There are a number of risk elements beyond those which are reflected in an option-adjusted statistic.

As the efficiency of the securitized-asset markets improves, it becomes harder to find above average yields readily, so you must work to find them. Creating your own models will shed a great deal more light not only on the risks but also on possibilities of superior returns flowing from professional investment management.

One last point, and here I pay tribute to Peter Lynch and his book *One Up on Wall Street* (Penguin Books, 1990). It is always easier to make a purchase decision than a sell decision. Once a security is in a portfolio, it is easy to forget about it. There are accounting implications. What will be the impact of a sale on book yield in the portfolio? There are capital-gain and -loss tax issues. There may be regulatory and surplus issues. In order to function in ways that maximize economic return and the decision making of a portfolio manager, there should be some measure of freedom from such constraints. To this point our performance in the relatively new field of securitized assets has not been unduly inhibited. Hopefully, it will stay that way, despite concerns voiced recently about derivatives in Washington and elsewhere. Active professional management on the investor side is a key to success in this field of investment.

10

The Role of Pension Funds and Other Investors in Securitized Debt Markets

Laurence D. Fink

Let me begin with a few general comments about securitization. Reduced to its essence, securitization is really a form of arbitrage. The slicing and dicing of cash flows and credit risks are a way to close the gap between less efficient debt markets and more efficient capital markets and to profit on the differentials that exist. As the level of understanding has grown on the part of originators, Wall Street professionals, and investors, the securitized markets have become more sophisticated. Understanding of option risk and the impact of negative convexity on yield and total return has risen markedly, and it must rise further.

Having said that, and having spent thirteen years on the Wall Street side of the market, I must add that the Street often works in a way adverse to the interests of investors. I am reminded about the old story of a poker game. If you sit in a game and after fifteen minutes you do not know who the patsy is, you are. The slicing and dicing of cash flows on securitized product by Wall Street at times seems to live off the naïveté of the patsy on the investor side.

Securitization can be viewed as a type of manufacturing. It involves changes, combinations, and recombinations of existing products and debt instruments into new forms. The process of materials conversion is similar to what an automobile manufacturer does in creating a car from steel, plastics, and other materials. Wall Street, by cutting up the cash flows emanating from debt instruments, is also in the business of manufacturing new products. The big problem is it does not give a five-year warranty on parts and labor. Its role is to package and sell, package and sell issues. The underwriting risk it takes disappears in a matter of days.

The major responsibility for understanding and evaluating risk falls on the institutional investors who buy the securities. It is imperative, therefore, that investors understand that their goals and the goals of the manufacturers of securitized product, Wall Street, are different and diverse. Wall Street does not want to see the security it sold ever again. And the government-sponsored enterprises (GSEs), which have been historically so instrumental to the development of securitized-product markets, do not either. The primary burden falls on investors. This is consistent with securities law, which has long placed the burden of investment risk on the buyer, who has the benefits of full disclosure in appropriate documents. So long as there is no buy-back guarantee, Wall Street and the GSEs will continue the process of packaging and securitizing assets.

Securitization has created fundamental changes in the role financial institutions play in financing the needs of businesses and households in America. Securitization of home mortgage debt, which began in the late 1970s, for example, accelerated the disintermediation of the savings and loan institutions. In one sense it filled the vacuum created by the failure of the thrifts to keep pace with loan demand. In another sense, it probably deepened the thrift crisis. Securitization of automobile loans, dating back to 1984, owed its early growth to the fact that the auto companies, which once enjoyed the highest credit ratings were being downgraded by Standard and Poor's and Moody's. Foreign competition at the manufacturing level and record delinquencies on automobile loans to consumers deteriorated the quality of their balance sheets and denied them access to cheap financing. So, they used the auto instalment paper as collateral and issued securitized car loans, which became known by the acronym, CARS. The process of meeting financing needs through securitization has expanded into additional fields with considerable rapidity. It seems to be most successful in markets where there is a vacuum, a shortage of funds and very high financing costs.

Three Requirements for Securitization

In my view, three conditions were necessary to convert securitization from a concept into a viable and powerful market reality capable of attracting pension funds and other institutional investors. These are (1) changes in securities laws and the legal investment powers of institutions, (2) changes in computer technology, and (3) changes in investor understanding regarding securitization.

Changes in securities laws were critical. For pension fund investors, changes in the labor laws governing their investment powers and in ERISA laws were necessary for participation in the field. In the past, pension funds were prohibited from buying securities collateralized by real estate. There were no such things as securities collateralized by real estate available in the market prior to 1970. Such investments were not in the excluded category of investments. They simply were not on the list at all. Thus, we were essentially breaking new ground. Laws had to be changed to permit investment in real estate securities, a new investment class, not only on the federal level, but often state by state.

The initial mortgage securities were offered under a legal form called a grantor trust. The grantor trust is a passively managed instrument. Once created, it cannot be changed through management. This creates severe limitations for investors interested in cash flows with greater predictability than is possible under a thirty-year, fixed-rate residential mortgage, especially one without any prepayment penalty. We had to move away from the limited grantor trust. New forms of trust agreements were designed over time, and the implications of each of these had to be negotiated with the appropriate committees of Congress, the Labor Department, the Internal Revenue Service, the nation's bank, thrift, and insurance regulators, and the accounting profession.

Legal issues aside, the economic risks presented by the mortgage as an investment vehicle proved a daunting challenge. The key issue was duration. During the 1970s and early 1980s securities backed by thirty-year mortgage collateral were traded on an industry convention that assumed they had a twelve-year life. This figure was based on academic studies of the experience of the Department of Housing and Urban Development (HUD) with FHA loans. Everyone knew that the twelve-year convention was a fictitious convention, and we all "guessed" at the true life and traded on our guesses. In 1983, a First Boston researcher came up with the term *HTG yield*, honest-to-goodness yield. He determined you could track prepayments on loan pools, and when you did, on the basis of the loans in the pool you would come up with an array of likely maturities, some longer than twelve years and many shorter. Different average life characteristics could be assigned to different pools. He determined further that you could divide the cash flows into predictable classes with reasonable certainty and identify different option-adjusted-spread characteristics as well. A breakthrough was at hand. We were moving to a new level in the development of securitization.

Why did it take until 1983 to begin to investigate the bifurcation of cash flows and the possible creation of collateralized mortgage obligations (CMOs)? One big reason is that we did not have the technology, the computer power, to do it. In the early 1980s, several Wall Street firms invested in personal computers and the talent to run them. The availability of these technical tools enabled us to take pools of mortgages and find ways to cut the cash flows up into new securities. We did not, however, sit down one day and say, "Let's carve up these cash flows and try to create a CMO. There is going to be a lot of investor demand, and we will make a lot of money." The ultimate buyers of mortgage security product during the late 1970s and early 1980s were the thrifts. They were happy with the rudimentary GNMA pass-through securities and the Freddie Mac issues. The development of the market of alternative buyers from among the institutional investor community brought us face-to-face with different client needs and the defects in our product offerings. Even as the new products were developed, sales volume was not great. More was needed.

This third element in the market development process was education. Trying to explain why mortgage securities—rated double-A or triple-A and priced at 150 and 300 basis points above U.S. Treasury obligations—were a good investment was not easy. And, after working through the client objections, you would find that you had problems with the ERISA rules or labor laws, so you had to go back to the drawing board. A common challenge was whether the security, if it involved Freddie Mac or Fannie Mae, was to be considered a real estate investment or a government agency obligation.

The duration challenge, the uncertain life characteristics of the thirty-year mortgage proved a monumental frustration to anyone seeking to sell mortgage product to an investor other than a thrift. Institutional investors would say, "I cannot own anything that has a final maturity of thirty years, even if it has a true life of five years." By 1983, thanks to computer technology and research into the history of mortgage payment streams, we were able to create multiclass securities, the beginnings of CMOs. The success of this process led to the packaging of securities in ways that fit the needs of the new investors and overcame market objections.

When the first multitranche collateralized mortgage obligation was created in 1983, the birth was not a smooth one. Freddie Mac at that time had a private letter ruling from the Internal Revenue Service permitting it to manipulate cash flows within a grantor trust. We called the resulting security a guaranteed mortgage certificate (GMC). The first issue was for $1 billion and to that point would be the second biggest public securities offering in the history of financial markets. Within one hour of the filing the U.S. Treasury stopped the issuance, saying it was an illegal offering. They rescinded their private letter ruling and said a grantor trust cannot be manipulated, even though Freddie Mac had previously received approval to do so. This is not a fun day in your career. Apparently the White House wanted to have the glory of liberalizing the securities laws to help housing and objected to an agency beating it to the punch. It planned to sponsor something called REMIC (Real Estate Mortgage Conduit) legislation, something that took four more years.

So, there you are with Freddie Mac having bought a billion dollars of mortgages. Basically what we did was to take the prospectus, scratch out GMC and write in CMO. This had a significant impact on Freddie Mac. A multitranche security was issued but without the desired tax pass-through features. The CMO was a collateralized debt offering, not a sale of assets.

The passage of the REMIC legislation in 1987 was vital to the type of securitized mortgage markets we enjoy today. The mortgage trust could not only manipulate cash flows but also get sales treatment for tax purposes. Large issuers entered the market, conduit companies developed, and the size of issues grew measurably.

One further point: institutional investing is not what we call absolute investing. It is basically relative investing. Performance on a portfolio is measured relative to an accepted index. Investors use a Salomon or Shearson-Lehman aggregate index as their performance measuring stick. These indexes contain all the fixed-income, dollar-denominated securities traded in the United States capital markets. Relative investing created another challenge for real estate securities. Until 1985, there was no mortgage securities index to serve as a performance benchmark. Thus, a traditional pension fund manager used to competing against a bond index was very, very reluctant to put mortgage securities in his portfolio unless he was absolutely confident they would outperform the index securities. Because mortgage securities were not part of the norm, the portfolio manager who bought into the sector early was taking a special risk with his investment committee and possibly his career.

The Wall Street answer was twofold. First, we used technology to create multiclass investment instruments that looked and acted more like bonds and delivered more predictable yields and total returns. Second, we invested in investor education. Investor seminars were conducted, research pieces disseminated, conferences hosted, and sales calls made in record numbers. The residential mortgage market was huge and worthy of the considerable effort given to it. The support received from the government-sponsored enterprises, Freddie Mac and Fannie Mae, in investor education was considerable. To bring securitization to its present state took a tremendous amount of plain hard work—major investments in technology, investor education, and legislative and regulatory work. If there was a master plan, it was to meet the needs of our institutional investor clients through the vehicle of residential mortgage debt.

The Role of Government-Sponsored Enterprises

It is important to understand that the role of Freddie Mac and Fannie Mae historically has been to nurture housing. They were to support the efforts of the thrift industry and mortgage bankers to provide home ownership at a lower cost to the general population of the United States. These agencies were not created by Congress to help investors. Now, the evolution of the securitized mortgage markets has created major concerns among institutional investors. Uncertainties are widening spreads on mortgage securities over Treasuries. The markets have become highly complex. Derivatives occupy more and more discussion time among investment committees and boards of directors. If the government-sponsored enterprises are to accomplish their primary mission, they must recognize their responsibility, as issuers of $1.3 trillion of securities collateralized by mortgages, to the investors who purchase and hold them. The investors need and deserve to have information throughout the life of the loan pools they own about the performance of these securities.

Problems Facing Investors

The first problem is responding to the need of institutional investors for reliable and timely information on the complex securitized issues. This must be available not only at time of the original issue but also on a continuing basis. Securities firms like Salomon, First Boston, or Merrill Lynch are the manufacturers and determine the makeup of the various product tranches. It is their responsibility, I submit, to provide information on these products throughout the life of the asset. They do not. In addition, the GSEs should provide more information to investors who hold the mortgage securities based on pools of their guaranteed collateral. Without more information the securitized markets will suffer, and the home buyers are likely to pay more for mortgage credit than they otherwise would.

Accurate and consistent pricing of mortgage securities product is a second major problem for institutional investors. Many investors must mark their investment holding to market on a regular basis. For open-end mutual funds, that pricing occurs daily and within an hour or so of the close of trading. If the pricing is wrong, fund customers have the right to say so and claim they were harmed by the bad prices, if necessary in court. Currently, it is very difficult to price precisely on a daily basis the thousands of unique mortgage tranches held by institutions. Some are quite illiquid. Although market participants talk about using option-adjusted spreads, I can tell you if you go to five Wall Street firms and take their "options models," you will get five different prices for the same issue. In fact, in my opinion the use of options models incorporating prepayment assumptions can be characterized as the full employment act for Wall Street. Hundreds of people with Ph.D.'s and other talents from great universities are making very good livings doing quantitative work creating models that do not work. The firms are all proud of their models, but they do not meet the client's need for timely, reliable, and consistent pricing.

My recommendation to the Securities and Exchange Commission (SEC), which has become highly concerned with this pricing challenge, is to take the initiative and set up a national pricing clearinghouse to gather and disseminate prices each day for all publicly traded mortgage-backed and other asset-backed securities. The new organization, a cooperative funded by assessing each issue a few basis points at origination, would gather prices of issues from all firms active in the market and from this data disseminate official industry prices at the end of the day. The technology to do this exists. What we need is the full appreciation of the value to the market of reliable and consistent pricing. If we had such market information early in 1994, problems like those afflicting Granite Capital would not happen. The losses in that firm's portfolio of $600 million did not happen in one week. The erosion of value occurred over some time but was masked by poor and inadequate pricing.

What the pricing service could do is take the average of the four or five best industry models and have a committee set the standard to be followed. Then, once a quarter it would rebalance or reset the standard. The key point is that you would have one measurement tool being used by everyone in the market. As an investment manager today I am required to follow the Salomon Bond Index. They change securities all the time, and I must rebalance my portfolio. Like the SEC, some may believe there is a right price. Keep in mind there is no right price. What you have is a price based on an option-adjusted spread built on a series of assumptions. As long as you have a standard that all market participants live by and authoritatively modify that standard as necessary, you will have more continuity and consistency in pricing, better markets, and better investor protection. Even if you do not agree with that price, you can trade off that convention or number in a consistent manner. The standard will give rationality to the market.

An appropriate role for the SEC in the mortgage securities field is the encouragement of a new centralized pricing cooperative for securitized assets. The manufacturing process through which Wall Street has created derivative securities flowing from collateralized asset pools has made significant progress. It has helped markets be more efficient and benefited both borrowers and investors. Prepayment risk, default risk, and other risks can be managed, provided they are priced properly, marked to market on a regular basis. Action on a common pricing standard should be the first order of business.

The Promise in Commercial Real Estate Securitization

First, let us review a bit of history. During the late 1980s we were asked many times to securitize commercial real estate debt. Offered a pool of assets totalling $100 million or more, we would package them and cut up the cash flows into tranches that we thought would meet investors' needs. When we took the deal back to the potential issuer, we would be told he could not do the deal without taking a 5 to 10 percent loss. Commercial real estate was being financed in ways that were totally separated from the global capital markets. Property prices were being driven by financing, not underlying values.

Today, in the mid-1990s, a new market has developed, and securitization is a primary factor in reliquifying real property markets. This has occurred because real estate prices have declined, because rating agencies understand commercial property better, and because the Resolution Trust Corporation (RTC) has demonstrated that investors do have an appetite for attractively priced securities. Commercial real estate can be packaged and sold today because it is responding to the pricing and clearing mechanism of the capital markets. In 1993, $40.3 billion of real estate assets were securitized successfully. Securitization met investors' needs.

Why are investors interested in the commercial product? The capital rules under which financial institutions operate are an important factor. Take insurance companies. When an insurance company owns a piece of real estate its regulatory rules say it must have 3 percent capital to support that investment holding. If it owns a rated mortgage security, down to a triple-B grade, the capital requirements would be only .3 percent. That is a tenfold difference. In essence, an insurance company today can hold ten times more securitized commercial real estate than underlying real estate for the same amount of capital. Capital requirements are going to be a major driver of securitized investment. Furthermore, the ERISA rules governing pension fund investment that currently prohibit investment by pension funds in commercial mortgage securities will be changed in the foreseeable future.

Commercial real estate securities have a big advantage over residential securities in that you can have call protection against prepayments. They can look and taste like a corporate bond to a much greater extent. In underwriting a commercial pool, the underwriting process focuses on credit risk, as with a corporate bond, not on cash flows. There is close to a trillion dollars of commercial real estate in the U.S. Given the necessary changes of law, the development of analytic talent, and the education of institutional investors, the growth can be huge. Early investors are enjoying spreads from seventy-five to two hundred basis points over similarly rated corporate bonds. Such returns will attract attention.

A word should be said about foreign institutional investors. The Japanese and certain European investors have been on-again, off-again participants in securitized markets. They have been most active in purchasing GNMA full-faith-and-credit paper and GSE securities. The motive behind these investments is once again regulatory capital requirements. Under the international Basel treaties governing the capital requirements of financial institutions, investments in full-faith-and-credit obligations of governments require no capital. GNMAs that enjoy a premium over Treasuries and require no capital become attractive. Fannie Mae and Freddie Mac issues have a risk weighting of only 20 percent of the requirement that would fall to a corporate bond. So, they too, with higher yields have attraction. Over time the role of foreign institutions in our market place will grow. At Blackrock we manage from $800 million to $1 billion of funds for Japanese institutions alone.

What about the traditional American financial institutions, banks and life insurance companies? What will their role be in this competitive, securitized world? Are banks and insurance companies going to be the next thrifts in the next round of financial distress? There is a good probability that will happen. Banks have enjoyed record profits during the last few years because the Federal Reserve has allowed them to do so. The steep yield curve combined with interest-rate swaps that do not cost capital and some one-time cost cutting have produced record profits. However, as the yield curve flattens, as it is doing now, and as banks with higher costs and capital requirements seek to compete for ownership of securitized assets, they will see margins erode. Unless there is a huge increase in business loans and senior debt lending, banks are likely to find themselves asset starved. Already there are signs that they have too much capital. Some are buying back stock. Others are increasing dividends. Earning a decent return on equity becomes difficult as their primary asset sources move directly from originator to investor through securitized capital markets.

In my view, senior bank debt is a prime candidate for securitization. The huge revolving credit lines of the type announced by IBM and Chemical Bank in early 1994 and syndicated among hundreds of banks is a case on point. Some mutual fund managers, such as the Van Kampen Group, already offer prime loan trust funds which offer floating rate loans to business corporations. This is just a beginning. As bank lending rates rise over this cycle, the opportunity to grow such funds and in the process outcompete banks can become a huge opportunity for enterprising loan packagers and securitizers.

Summing Up

Securitization is probably the biggest single change affecting our financial landscape during the past sixty years, since the Great Depression. The implications of this linking of the creators of debt and the global capital markets has monumental implications for banks, thrifts, and insurance companies. It broadens greatly the investment options available to institutional investors and will change how they buy, monitor, and price the assets in portfolios. The securitized markets are, at best, in their adolescent stage. Both their growth rate and the learning curve necessary to produce mature judgments about them will see rapid development. The contributions of technology and the people who can operate it will grow significantly. Success in these markets, which initially went to those who could bifurcate cash flows and innovate product offerings, is more likely to flow to those who can evaluate the underlying credit risk that lies within the various manufactured securities in good times and bad, over high and low interest-rate cycles. A new breed of specialists are likely to arise in the form of specialized investment advisors who will position themselves between the manufacturers in Wall Street and institutional investors. Freddie Mac and Fannie Mae, it is to be hoped, will broaden the amount and timeliness of information on issues bearing their guarantees, and the SEC will encourage the creation of a central pricing cooperative to provide the authoritative valuation of securitized assets necessary for fair and orderly markets.

11

The Place of Securitization in the Financial System: Implications for Banking and Monetary Policy

Susan M. Phillips

Capital market activity has surged in the last few years, largely because of three factors, improved technology, improved communications, and advances in financial theory. The first two of these factors have lowered trading costs and along with the third have helped to foster the development of many innovative kinds of financial instruments. Securitization is an important part of this development in capital markets. At the end of 1993, outstanding asset-backed securities amounted to just under 20 percent of nonfederal, nonfinancial debt outstanding. By contrast, in 1985 that figure was only about 8 percent.

This essay covers three securitization topics. First, I discuss the effect of securitization on commercial banks. Then, I discuss the effect of securitization on the Federal Reserve and its conduct of monetary policy. Finally, I discuss the effect of securitization on the Federal Reserve and its role as a bank supervisor.

The Effect of Securitization on Commercial Banks

Securitization represents an especially important development for banks. Since more assets can now be regularly traded in convenient forms, the role of financial intermediaries has changed. In short, the line between loans and securities has blurred as more loans can be readily transformed into securities. Banks have been key participants in this ongoing process, both as suppliers of assets to be securitized and as holders of mortgage-backed and asset-backed securities and derivatives on those securities.

I would like to thank Thomas Brady for his assistance in the preparation of this article. The views in this paper are solely those of the author and do not reflect the opinions of the Board of Governors of the Federal Reserve System or its staff.

The growth of securitization and capital market activity more generally has been reflected in a decline in bank assets as a share of total nonfinancial debt. This share fell from 40 percent in 1985 to 30 percent in 1993. This does not, however, necessarily mean that there were fewer loans or that there is a reduced role for banks in the lending process. In fact, data from the Department of Housing and Urban Development show that banks' share of mortgage loan originations is higher in the 1990s than it was in the second half of the 1980s. So even though securitization has taken a lot of assets off the balance sheets of banks, banks are still originating an increasing proportion of mortgage loans. Not surprisingly, in view of the growing importance of securitization, originations by mortgage bankers have also increased, in fact by more than banks. The share accounted for by thrifts has declined, as has that by life insurance companies.

Securitization expands the sources of loanable funds, putting downward pressure on yields. This lower borrowing cost is an obvious advantage for borrowers. At the same time, the lower yields make these assets less attractive for banks and other intermediaries. There is another, offsetting, effect though. The negative impact of the lower yields is offset to some degree by the fact that these assets are tradable in liquid markets. In addition, the advent of securitization and derivatives has spawned a variety of new financial instruments that fill out various market niches. To the extent that banks find some of these new assets attractive on the basis of various combinations of their liquidity and risk characteristics, then even if yields are lower than before, securitization may actually serve to boost the size of banks' balance sheets.

Indeed, banks in recent years have added considerable volumes of mortgage-backed pass-through securities and collateralized mortgage obligations to their balance sheets. Since 1988, the proportion of mortgage-backed securities as a percentage of bank assets has tripled from 3 percent to 9 percent. In 1993 banks acquired $29 billion in mortgage-backed securities, and as of the end of 1993 they held about 22 percent of all mortgage-backed securities outstanding.

In some sense, it might seem odd that banks would be large investors in securitized products. Banks specialize in credit analysis and are the natural investor in assets that require individual credit analysis. This is not the case with mortgage-backed or asset-backed securities, where the credit rating has been done by the rating agencies. There are two major reasons why banks do invest in these securities. The first reason is, to the extent that a bank's customers are not interested in taking out new loans, banks will seek out capital market investments. The second reason involves banks' capital requirements. Banks have much higher capital requirements on loans than on securities. So if a bank is under pressure to improve its capital ratio, then there is an incentive to invest in securities. Now that many banks have shored up their balance sheets, they will have less incentive to invest in securities and a greater incentive to originate new loans.

The growth of securitization and the advent of derivatives has many positive implications for banking. By facilitating unbundling and specialization, securitization allows banks to operate more efficiently and more profitably. Banks can originate more loans than would have otherwise been the case. This is particularly true for mortgages and consumer credit. In 1993, banks originated an estimated $258 billion in residential mortgages. Such mortgages on bank balance sheets, however, rose by only $51 billion. It is probably safe to say that many of the loans that banks securitize would not have been originated had the banks been required to keep them on their balance sheets.

That banks can originate and securitize loans enables them to more fully exploit their special expertise of analyzing the credit worthiness of borrowers. Credit analysis, the intermediation function that banks have traditionally performed so well, can sometimes be difficult for capital markets. By eliminating the need to provide the financing for all of its loans, securitization enables banks to apply their credit analysis expertise on many more loans. This can boost earnings and lower the cost of accumulating capital. Further, this can enable banks to seek out other assets to hold, particularly assets that are not easily securitizable.

This is not to say that securitization will not lead to more credit analysis being performed by the capital market. To some extent, securitization, the emergence of new technology, and the improved skills of rating agencies are bound to erode the banking industry's position as the best source of credit analysis. More entities will go directly to the capital market. Nevertheless, there is room for both banks and the capital market. Banks will be strong competitors with a particular advantage, as always, in small business finance and other areas in which direct access to the capital markets is difficult. But credit markets will be more competitive.

This competition will be beneficial for consumers, though sometimes it might not be readily apparent. Consider the case of credit cards. Interest rates on credit cards have dropped over the years, but the average rate of change might perhaps be described as glacial. Looking deeper into the credit card market, though, we can see a lot of product differentiation. Different banks offer different kinds of cards to different kinds of customers. There is a lot of competition, though it often does not tend to be on the basis of the interest rate offered.

Increased competition will lead to some consolidation of the banking industry. We have already seen significant mergers and takeovers, and we have seen a good bit of the thrift industry disappear. The downsizing that has occurred in the banking industry is possibly, in part, motivated by excess capacity. This entails some dislocations. But this is typical of other large industries that go through reengineering processes in order to find their new niche and to become more efficient. Banks will focus on their comparative advantage. This will entail the provision of quality customer services and other things that the capital markets are less able to deliver. Banks are grappling with these issues now.

By giving banks more ways to adjust their balance sheets, securitization has made their assets more liquid. This has proved helpful to banks in particular circumstances and in particular periods of time. For example, in the late 1980s and the early 1990s, banks were under considerable pressure—both from the financial market and from regulators—to strengthen their capital ratios. For many banks, the cheapest way to do this was to shrink their assets through securitization. In fact, these capital ratio pressures likely served as an impetus to the development of techniques to securitize credit card receivables.

A relatively recent innovation has been the use of securitization in the commercial mortgage market. This new market has facilitated the removal of subpar loans from banks' balance sheets. Further, we have seen a dramatic improvement in the delinquency rates for commercial real estate loans as a result of the ability to securitize these loans.

Coupled with the developments in asset-backed securities markets have been developments in the derivatives markets. Banks have been able to exploit the derivatives markets in ways that benefit both themselves and their customers. Banks use derivatives to reduce risk by hedging their own exposures. For example, a recent Federal Reserve survey of senior loan officers indicates that many banks are using prime versus LIBOR-basis swaps to protect their prime-based loans. Banks also use derivatives to offer new products to their customers. For example, on the lending side, customers can be offered floating-rate loans with ceilings. Banks also are offering new types of deposits, for instance, deposits with returns linked to the performance of equity markets.

Of course, though derivatives have enhanced banks' abilities to manage their portfolios and to generate fee income, these derivatives are obviously very complicated and in some cases might entail considerable risk. So the growth in the derivatives market heightens the need to monitor and supervise their use by banks.

The Effect of Securitization on the Federal Reserve and on the Conduct of Monetary Policy

Monetary policy is carried out by affecting the supply of reserves relative to the banking system's demand for those reserves. Therefore, it is natural to ask whether the growing importance of securitization, and the flow of funds that bypass the banking system, is going to affect the Federal Reserve's ability to conduct monetary policy. This is a matter of great interest to the Federal Reserve.

In general, monetary policy actions affect interest rates and exchange rates, influencing economic activity over the short run and determining the rate of inflation over the long run. How is this done? There are three channels of monetary transmission that are generally identified. The first is the interest rate and exchange rate channel, the second is the credit or lending channel, and the third channel is through direct credit restrictions. Some channels are more important in some countries, and some are more important in others. Though theorists argue about this, I think that there is general agreement that interest rates are the primary channel for monetary policy in the U.S. Hence, my comments will focus primarily on the interest rate channel.

Most efforts to carry out monetary policy are done with open market operations. These operations expand or contract the volume of reserves that banks and other depositories can use to fulfill their statutory reserve requirements. Since the Federal Reserve controls the supply of reserves, it is able to exert considerable influence over the price of those reserves, the price being the interest rate on overnight interbank loans, commonly known as the federal funds rate. Changes in monetary policy, then, are generally reflected in changes in the trading range of the federal funds rate.

Though the Federal Reserve's most direct influence is on the federal funds rate, considerable influence is exerted on other key interest rates as well through arbitrage. This is particularly true with respect to short-term interest rates. Long-term interest rates are affected by changes in the federal funds rate, but the effect here is through expected future short-term rates. In addition, long-term rates are influenced by expectations of future demands for credit, expectations regarding inflation, and other types of risk. So the relation of monetary policy to long-term rates is much looser than the relation to short-term rates.

Three issues are involved in the question of how securitization affects the Federal Reserve's ability to conduct monetary policy. The first has to do with a possible decrease or diminution in the ability of the Federal Reserve to affect interest rates through open market operations in the manner just described, by buying and selling securities to affect reserve levels. The second issue has to do with the impact of securitization on how the economy reacts to changes in monetary policy. The third issue has to do with the impact of capital market innovations on the behavior of the monetary aggregates that the Federal Reserve uses as guides in implementing monetary policy.

With respect to the ability of the Federal Reserve to affect interest rates through open market operations, the Federal Reserve clearly maintains the ability to control the federal funds rate within fairly narrow limits. Moreover, despite the relative shrinkage of the banking system, there is no evidence that the link between the federal funds rate and other short-term market rates or exchange rates has diminished. Banks are still quite active in a variety of financial markets and are a very large presence in other markets. Changes in the actual and the expected cost of reserves are still quickly and efficiently transmitted, via arbitrage, to other market rates.

Now, one could conduct a mental experiment and envision a world in which it is feasible and profitable to securitize progressively more and more bank assets, to the point where banks originate but do not hold loans. If all bank assets disappeared into the capital markets, then of course there would be no bank liabilities either, and hence no demand for reserves. In such a world, the Federal Reserve's current techniques for influencing market interest rates would not function. I do not, however, think that this will happen. Banks offer the only absolutely safe, insured source of demand and savings deposits, and it is likely that these instruments will continue to serve the public's transactions needs. Moreover, there is every reason to believe that the public's need for transaction and other types of liquid balances will grow with economic activity. The capital market developments that promote securitization have no direct implications for the public's demand for such bank liabilities.

Another factor influencing the demand for bank reserves is the fact that only the Federal Reserve can offer absolutely safe and final clearing of accounts among banks. This implies that the demand for reserve and clearing balances is likely to remain large. Therefore, banks' arbitrage activities in the federal funds market will remain more than sufficient to ensure that changes in the supply of reserves to the market via open market operations will have implications for other types of short-term rates. For these reasons, it seems unlikely that the Federal Reserve will encounter technical problems in implementing monetary policy with open market operations any time soon.

Consider the second issue, how the economy reacts to changes in monetary policy. In particular, what are the implications of the change in the institutional setting brought about by securitization? From this perspective the development of securitization can be viewed as a further evolution away from the institutional setup that we had not so many years ago, a world with deliberately established impediments to interest-rate movements and the flow of loanable funds. In particular, I am referring to interest-rate ceilings on banks and thrift deposits that were established under Regulation Q.

Regulation Q resulted in periodic episodes of disintermediation. This was when economic activity would push market interest rates above the Regulation Q limits. This would cause a flow of funds out of banks and thrifts and into market instruments. There were several such episodes in the 1960s and 1970s. These episodes had a particularly heavy impact on the availability of funds to the residential mortgage market. Banks and thrifts were essentially out of the mortgage business, and mortgage credit dried up. As a consequence, housing was particularly sensitive to periods of monetary stringency. With the abolition of these interest-rate ceilings, the impact of monetary restraint is more widespread; housing no longer takes the full brunt of monetary policy. The economy's reaction to changes in monetary policy is smoother and is spread over more sectors. Securitization extends this development by making financial flows still less dependent on specialized lenders. This improves the economy's adaptability to periods of stress. In contrast to the Regulation Q experience, consider the economic contraction of the late 1980s and early 1990s. The contraction of the thrift industry had little or no sustained spillover effects into the residential housing market. The capital markets were able to step in, via the banks and the mortgage bankers, to fill the void created by the contraction of the thrift industry.

As a consequence of these market liberalizations, interest rates will probably have to go higher than was once the case in order to have a restraining influence. And although monetary theorists may argue about it, I would say that the lags probably are going to be longer and more variable.

The institutional changes of securitization also have implications for the so-called credit channel of monetary policy. The credit channel is deemed distinct from the interest-rate and exchange-rate channel and focuses on the banking industry's role as a unique source of credit. The idea is that as monetary policy adds or removes reserves from the banking system, then the set of borrowers who rely exclusively on bank credit will be directly affected by the availability, or lack of availability, of loanable funds. Thus, even apart from its influence on interest rates, a change in monetary policy would lead to a reallocation of credit across the economy. This is probably a less accepted channel of monetary transmission. In any case, to the extent that securitization opens up capital markets and reduces the set of borrowers who must rely solely on banks, the effects of monetary policy through this credit channel are mitigated.

Now, consider the impact of securitization on the monetary aggregates that are used by the Federal Reserve to guide its policy. Here, the effects of securitization and other capital market developments, most notably the growth of mutual funds, are clear. With deposits flowing out of banks and into these other assets, recent money growth has been below what the historical experience would suggest it would be. Put another way, increases in the ratio of gross domestic product to the broader monetary aggregates has been exceptionally rapid. This ratio, called the velocity of money, has risen under circumstances when it previously would have been expected to be flat or declining.

The monetary aggregates have been less useful guides to monetary policy in the last couple of years than they used to be. There is still information in the monetary aggregates, but their movement needs to be interpreted carefully. They cannot be relied on as much as they once were as guides to monetary policy.

It remains to be seen whether the change in the behavior of monetary aggregates is temporary or permanent. That the last few years have been a period of learning and adaptation for banks and their customers suggests that the current behavior of the aggregates may be temporary. Further, time will tell whether the flow out of M2 and into bond and stock mutual funds is a permanent phenomenon. Recent long-term interest-rate increases may remind the public about the distinction between the safety and liquidity of bank deposits relative to bond and equity funds.

The Effect of Securitization on the Federal Reserve and Its Role as a Bank Supervisor

Over the years, banks have become more involved in the expanding array of derivatives and other capital market instruments. It is important for the Federal Reserve and the bank examiners to understand capital markets and to make sure that the banks understand the subtleties of these markets. Further, there is a need to understand the link between the growth of securitization and derivatives and the potential for systemic risk to the banking system and the financial system more generally.

Supervisory efforts have focused on a number of issues. The first concerns managerial oversight of risk management. We want to make sure that senior management is actively involved in the oversight of the risk management systems. The second concerns independent management review of the risk management process. Are experts independent of the trading function looking at the internal models that banks use for risk management purposes? Is someone else assessing whether these models contain realistic and up-to-date economic parameters? A related issue involves the auditing of the risk management and internal control processes. How do the firms go about assessing credit risk, market risk, liquidity risk, operational risk, and legal risk?

Disclosure and accounting standards are also key issues. Do financial statements contain adequate information about the risk being assumed? This information is for both investors and regulators. I do not think that adequate accounting and reporting standards are in place yet, but they are in process. Bank regulators and the Financial Accounting Standards Board are currently working on issues in this area.

Another issue concerns whether there is an appropriate level of protection for unsophisticated parties—be they institutions or individuals. The Federal Reserve's primary focus has been on overseeing banks' activities, not the activities of banks' customers. There are, however, important questions concerning banks' responsibilities in assessing whether a transaction is appropriate for a particular customer.

Of course, after a bank or a dealer discloses all of the risks of a particular transaction, it is going to be the customer that makes the decision. And if there is risk, there may be losses. Just as recent experience has shown that a lot of firms took on more debt than they should have, we will no doubt see firms enter into inappropriate transactions. Ultimately, however, risk management decisions will be made by customers.

Educational endeavors have been undertaken within the Federal Reserve and the government more generally. Both the comptroller of the currency and the Federal Reserve have supplied extensive information on derivatives. The private sector has also undertaken an educational campaign. For instance, the Group of 30 study contains very relevant guidance in terms of risk management for financial institutions.

The final area that the Federal Reserve has spent time on, and will probably spend more time on, is risk-based capital requirements. Changes have been made to the capital formula to take account of credit risk. Further, there are current proposals to make changes to account for interest-rate risk and market risk. This is a complicated process. This is an international market, and so the process involves negotiations with our counterparts in other countries. More will be heard about changes to the regulatory system for derivatives. Several bills have been offered in Congress and the General Accounting Office is preparing a report on derivatives.

In summary, securitization and the attendant changes in capital markets, including the development of derivatives, have been beneficial to the financial system and to the economy overall. But these changes have raised legitimate concerns. The Federal Reserve and other banking regulators have taken the supervisory and regulatory aspects of the derivatives markets seriously and have worked to assure that examiners have an adequate understanding of derivative transactions and related risks. Regulatory and accounting changes are also in process to address new types of instruments and risk management techniques. The more complex market environment and the possibility of systemic risk have also made the implementation of monetary policy and monitoring of the financial markets more challenging. But, overwhelmingly, the advantages in terms of fostering the efficient uses of savings and capital and the benefits to real economic growth have outweighed the problems.

12

The Use of Securitization by Investors and Issuers in International Markets

Marcia Myerberg

An appropriate first question is, how does one become a pioneer in international or global securitization? The answer is simple: Lew Ranieri asks, how would you like to create a secondary mortgage market in the United Kingdom? And you accept it as an interesting challenge. In 1985, at Salomon, we saw several forces coming together that indicated the United Kingdom, Europe, and other international markets were ripe for securitization.

The forces that gave impetus to global securitization appear in table 12.1. They are issuer demand, investor demand, and profit potential for Wall Street. In the United Kingdom, potential issuers were faced with new challenges, and securitization was capable of meeting them.

As to issuer demand, the international banking community, meeting in Basel, Switzerland, had come together and established worldwide capital standards for various types of risk assets that were held on bank balance sheets. These standards were to go into effect by 1992. As a consequence, banks and other regulated financial institutions around the globe would be required to manage their balance sheets to the new universal standards at a time when capital was in relatively short supply. There was also a growing need to manage liquidity because of gyrating interest rates. Securitization in the United States had proved to be a very efficient way of meeting such needs. It permitted an organization to raise money even though it was short of capital. It could create liquidity out of illiquid assets and serve as an efficient funding mechanism.

On the other side of the coin, there had to be an ample supply of funds and investor demand before any securities market could start. In the United States mortgage-backed securities had proved to be high-quality assets offering very attractive returns. In the United Kingdom we had to identify investors seeking high-quality assets with attractive returns and take that message to them.

Table 12.1
Global securitization impetus

• Issuer demand
    Basel Accords (capital adequacy ratios)
    Balance sheet/Liquidity management
    Efficient funding mechanism
• Investor demand
    High-quality assets with attractive returns
• Profit opportunity for Wall Street firms

Finally, there had to be a profit opportunity for Wall Street, and this is probably the primary reason Salomon ventured overseas. The United Kingdom provided us with an opportunity to cash in on the development expenses that went into the creation of the mortgage securities market in the United States.

The U.K. Experience

The United Kingdom, in 1985, had a $400 billion mortgage market. A market this size could benefit materially from a securitization effort, and an investment banker could achieve the economies of scale necessary for successful issuances without taking on the whole market. The legal system of the United Kingdom was based on the common law, as opposed to the civil law prevalent on the European continent. No enabling legislation was required to issue securities, and many of the techniques developed in U.S. markets could be exported, so to speak. Finally, the British spoke our language, or at least a form of our language. Thus, the basics could be put in place fairly quickly.

The home loan market was dominated by building societies, organizations that might be described as a cross between savings and loan associations and mutual savings banks. They were mutuals, depositor owned, not stockholder owned. They funded mortgage loans with deposits accumulated from savers and paid them interest on those savings accounts. A very interesting feature of the British system is that all the home loans were variable rate. The institutional exposure to interest-rate risk was minimal. In marked contrast, U.S. savings and loans had portfolios dominated by fixed-rate loans and were grievously exposed to interest-rate risk. The building society system totally dominated the home loan market. The capital markets were not used

Table 12.2
U.K. mortgage market, 1985

- $400 billion mortgage market
- Common law—common language
- Dominated by building societies
- Deposit-based funding—all variable rate
- No secondary market
- Low delinquency rates
- Thatcher government initiatives: Home ownership, privatization program, deregulation
- Disintermediation—mortgage queues
- Borrower need=Securitization opportunity

to fund mortgages, and there was no secondary mortgage market. The market was also very attractive because of its high quality, relatively high down payments, and very low delinquency rates. The Briton's home was, indeed, his castle, and defaults on mortgage loans were rare.

The Thatcher government was a strong advocate of home ownership. To increase it, the government sought to privatize what is called council housing, low-income rental housing, by giving renters an opportunity to buy their units on very attractive terms. The building societies were to participate in that financing. At the same time that it was pushing home ownership, the Thatcher government also privatized other government-owned businesses such as British Telecom. This action offered the public popular forms of investment other than savings deposits. Common stock and mutual fund investment rose in popularity. Shortly thereafter the government began a process of deregulating the financial system, in a manner similar to that which transpired in the United States. Disintermediation increased, and funds flowed directly from savers to capital market investments without passing through intermediaries.

These actions led to a shortage of mortgage funds from traditional outlets. Potential homebuyers found themselves queuing up for mortgage money, literally waiting in line at building societies for the opportunity to talk to a loan officer about the prospects of obtaining home loan funds. This supply-demand imbalance created a very attractive climate for the introduction of securitization into the United Kingdom (see table 12.2).

Table 12.3
U.K. capital markets, 1985

- No adverse government regulation
- Sterling floating-rate notes—unrated, unsecured debt of building societies
- Strong investor appetite for sterling floating-rate assets
- Limited supply due to funding restrictions
- Investor demand=Securitization opportunity

Conditions in the U.K. capital markets in 1985 are summarized in table 12.3. On the investor side, virtually the only sterling debt being issued was floating-rate notes offered by building societies to meet the loan demand. Even though these issues were unrated and unsecured debt, the investors loved them. They were of good quality. However, the supply was limited because of restrictions on the amount of money building societies could raise through borrowing. The shortage of new offerings and strong evidence of investor appetite for quality floating-rate product was highly favorable for the introduction of new products into the market.

These favorable conditions enabled us to bring securitization into the United Kingdom on an incoming tide. There was a supply vacuum to be filled at a time of rising demand. Since the United Kingdom had no counterpart to our government-sponsored enterprises, Freddie Mac and Fannie Mae, the concepts that were developed were driven by market forces. We created a company called "The Mortgage Corporation," which was both a primary mortgage lender making loans to home buyers and a funder of those loans through the issuance of mortgage-backed securities. Simply, we put together a private mortgage banking company and a conduit. We had to establish an alternative loan-origination mechanism to the building societies to get the product to securitize. Several U.K. companies also entered the market. In fact, Salomon securitized and sold mortgage securities for one of these issuers one month before The Mortgage Corporation issued securities. The first Mortgage Corporation deal was offered to the market in February 1987.

The issues one must deal with in pioneering a concept in a new market are interesting. For example, in the United States, we tie the borrowers' floating rate to a well-known and widely used index, like the one year Treasury rate. In the United Kingdom, mortgage rates floated, not off an index, but off the will of the lender. Individual boards of directors could decide to raise or lower their lending rates at will, and there were no floors or caps. How could we fit such conditions into a securitized product with investor appeal? The answer was to create a pay-through bond structure that adjusted every three months on the basis of a LIBOR index. We offered investors a three-month, fixed-rate note, and all notes adjusted every three months. The individual home loans were designed to float the same way. And, if they did not float at the indicated spread over LIBOR, we would put up cash to make up any shortfall. In this manner, we could continue to allow the setting of rates at will by the lender and still meet the demands of the investors and the rating agencies for certainty of cash flow.

The rating agency process raised additional structuring issues. The agencies had to be satisfied that the proposed structure would meet their requirements for timely payment of interest and ultimate payment of principal. Certainty of cash flows required credit enhancement from a third-party guarantor with the capital status to validate the desired rating. Without a Freddie Mac or Fannie Mae, we had to look to the insurance market in the United Kingdom and Europe for this support. In 1985, fortunately, there were a number of triple-A companies willing to write coverage on both the individual low-down-payment loans and first-loss coverage on the entire pool being securitized. Their premium costs were very low, too low, as subsequent events would indicate. The Standard and Poor's ratings were then forthcoming at the triple-A level.

By 1990, over $10 billion of floating-rate mortgage-backed securities had been issued from a standing start in 1987. That was an excellent launch of a new concept. The history of financial market concepts indicates that they do not grow in a straight upward direction. There are failures and learning experiences to go with the successes. Securitization in the United Kingdom was not an exception.

Salomon introduced mortgage banking companies into the United Kingdom at a time when the dominant home lenders, the building societies, had suffered deposit outflows and could not handle the loan demand. Historically, the building societies had an 85 to 90 percent market share of loan originations. The best way for them to continue to meet loan demand was to embrace the secondary market and securitization, but they chose not to do so. So, Salomon entered the primary mortgage market and began to originate home loans in volume, in order to have a product to securitize. Salomon was very definitely regarded as an invader by the local thrifts. When we launched a television advertising campaign and began to offer mortgages by mail, these were not welcomed acts.

By the fourth quarter of 1987, these new mortgage bankers and the commercial banks were originating 50 percent of the nation's home loans. The building societies determined to fight back. Over the next three years they cut loan rates aggressively and were able to do so because of a stock market crash in the United Kingdom that mirrored the 1987 crash in the U.S. markets. The small depositors, who had taken their money out of building societies to buy stocks, nervously sold shares and brought the funds back to the building societies, reliquifying them. The funds were available for aggressive lending, and they were so used.

In hindsight, the new breed of specialized mortgage bankers were overly aggressive in pursuing volume, commissions, and market share. By angering the building societies, they fomented a commercial war that involved both price cuts and the lowering of the quality of credit. The new lenders determined that they were not going to give back to building societies the market share they had captured through securitization. To compete, they cut quality. For example, they lowered underwriting standards by offering loans based on limited documentation—no credit or employment checks and quick appraisals to speed the loan process and qualify more borrowers.

At the same time, the chancellor of the exchequer undertook a national policy of lowering interest rates. In the summer of 1988, mortgage rates dipped below 10 percent for the first time in a decade. Consumers viewing the housing market saw it as a one-way bet. It could only go up. Lower rates made home ownership affordable, and lenders were competing aggressively to make loans. First-time home buyers, who now could qualify, rushed to get into the market, and existing homeowners sought to use their rising equity to move up the chain. Property prices rose to new peaks as speculative fever grew. Unfortunately, there was a paucity of information about the deterioration of the quality of the market. Because of this lack of information on delinquencies and similar measures, the good times went on too long and set the stage for a bust.

Then, the U.K. economy turned. The first-time home buyer, who qualified for a mortgage at 9.9 percent in 1988, was paying 14 percent by January 1990. The capital market yield curve was steeply inverted. The squeeze on first-time buyers and others who aggressively mortgaged their properties put pressures on house prices, and they collapsed. New buyers were scarce. By 1992, delinquencies for certain lenders reached 20 percent, an unheard-of number even in Texas during its troubled years, and foreclosures peaked as well. The mortgage insurers, who failed to price their product and take into account the catastrophic conditions now confronting the mortgage markets, suffered huge losses. When pool insurance issuance was suspended, the securitization market lost its primary technique for enhancing the credit of loan pools. In another disturbing development, National Home Loans, one of the new breed of mortgage bankers and private conduits, became involved in the BCCI scandal, which took it out of the market. Conditions were serious and deteriorating.

What else could possibly happen? At this very time, world banking regulators published their more restrictive international standards for capital, generally referred to as the Basel accords. Loans and securities were to receive significantly different capital risk weightings. In the United Kingdom, because of language translation problems, mortgage securities were mistakenly reported to have a 100 percent risk rating, whereas individual mortgage loans would have a 50 percent assessment. Even though the rules ultimately turned out to be the same for both, the market did not wait to react. The initial effect of the Basel accords on the appetite of investors for mortgage securities was seriously negative. The volume of new mortgage securities issues fell from a high of $4 billion in 1989 to only $500 million in 1992. Without an active funding source, the mortgage banking industry atrophied, and the building societies recaptured a 90 percent share of the decimated market.

What happened to the mortgage-backed securities market? Its authenticity and staying power were validated. Because of the large losses, the pool insurers and mortgage indemnity insurers suffered declines in their credit ratings. As a consequence, most of the issues that were rated triple-A were downgraded as well. This occurred under the weakest-link theory of the rating agencies. The rating of a particular security issue can be no higher than the rating of its weakest link. To overcome this problem, senior subordinated structures were introduced into the market. Acceptance was very good. Most investors prefer them because they eliminate event risk. You do not have to worry about the mortgage or the insurer being downgraded since the credit enhancement is provided through the securities structure itself.

The spreads on mortgage-backed securities widened from fifteen basis points over LIBOR at issuance to sixty basis points because of the downgrades and the Basel problem. The spreads moved back to twenty-five basis points after the confusion over the Basel capital requirements was straightened out.

The important point to remember is that the structures created to issue mortgage-backed securities held and weathered the storm. No investors suffered a shortfall. The cash flow continued. The mortgages paid, and where there was a default, the advancing mechanisms worked. All investors received their money on time and in full—with one exception. A subordinate National Home Loans piece missed payment once but caught up the next month. A key point is that there is still a very strong demand for these securities.

The Market to Date

Activity in the U.K. securitized market to date is summarized in table 12.4. Total issuances have reached $20 billion and cover not only first and second home loans but also commercial property leases, car loans, consumer loans, trade receivables, and bank loans. This is not bad for a market that is geographically the size of Minnesota! The Mortgage Corporation continued to be the largest issuer. The rating process is of vital importance. Without the oversight of the public rating agencies like Standard and Poor's and Moody's, I do not think the deals would have held up during the period of stress. Without agency insistence, the deals would not have been structured with adequate coverage to make it through the catastrophic-risk period. Looking ahead, I think future growth of securitization is likely to be driven by the need to manage balance sheets and create liquidity out of illiquid assets. One can expect virtually anything that has cash flow to be a candidate for securitization.

Table 12.4
U.K. issues to date

- 79 issues—$20 billion

- 74 floating rate notes, 5 fixed rate, 3 U.S. $ commercial paper programs

- 22 issuers—1 building society, 5 centralized lenders, 7 foreign banks, 2 clearing banks, 3 insurance companies, 3 auto finance companies, 1 finance company

- Largest issuer—The Mortgage Corporation (16 issues, $4.5 billion)

- All issues are rated by Standard and Poor's or Moody's

- Assets: First and second mortgages, commercial property leases, auto loans / receivables, unsecured consumer loans, trade receivables, bank loans

---

The Investor Base

One goal of the securitization process is to broaden the base of investors willing to buy assets in a specific market sector. Securitized assets offered good yields on high-quality assets, liquidity, diversification, and potential trading profits. Such appealing values attract new sources of funds to a market sector and lower borrower costs, thereby expanding the base market. This has occurred in the United States, and it has happened in the United Kingdom as well. Nonmortgage investors were attracted to the U.K. mortgage-backed securities market from outside that nation, as well as from within. It proved itself to be an international market. Tables 12.5 and 12.6 show the type of investors who were major purchasers of mortgage-backed securities and their geographic location.

Banks have purchased 45 percent of the mortgage-backed securities issued in the United Kingdom to date, with one major clearing bank holding about 30 percent of the outstandings. This bank is also a major purchaser of U.S. dollar mortgage securities. Corporations have 26 percent, insurance companies 12 percent, and other financial institutions 12 percent. Interestingly, the building societies hold only 5 percent of the U.K. mortgage-backed securities. But that 5 percent is very important because once building societies start investing, they are likely to start issuing. Since they originate 90 percent of the new home loans today, they hold the future growth of the market in their hands.

Table 12.5
U.K. mortgage-backed securities investor base by type

- Banks—45% (one U.K. clearing bank holds about 30% of the outstanding U.K. mortgage-backed securities)
- Corporations—26%
- Insurance companies—12%
- Other financial institutions—12%
- Building societies—5%

Table 12.6
U.K. mortgage-backed securities investor base by location

- United Kingdom—59%
- U.S.—20%
- Continental Europe—16%
- Far East—5%

You will not have a growing mortgage securities market unless building societies start issuing. The fact that they are now investing bodes well for the future.

As to geography, it is interesting to note that over 40 percent of the issues, all denominated in sterling, were sold to investors in other countries. Note, 20 percent of the investors were in the United States. Apparently, some Americans believe the yield is adequate to compensate for the currency risk. Or, those investors are U.S. companies that have a need for sterling assets and see mortgage-backed securities as high-quality repositories.

Summing up, we were able to take the securitization concepts developed in the United States to another country and have the basic framework work. The test in the United Kingdom demonstrates that our securitization concepts, the structure and framework, are sound. They can withstand catastrophic economic conditions and do what they promise. We also learned that good work can be undone by weak analysis of market conditions and poor management of credit risk. The market participants—mortgage bankers, investment bankers, real estate developers, and home buyers—all got ahead of themselves and created speculative excesses that led to poor investment performance and significant losses. But, the securitized structures survived quite well. Thus, one can conclude that the U.K. market will come back and that we will securitize much larger dollar volumes and a broader range of products for the institutions and people of that island kingdom.

The French Experience

The French market posed a very different set of issues to securitization from the British market. First, French law, based on the Napoleonic Code, was very different from American or English law. Therefore, enabling legislation was necessary before any product design or marketing decisions could be attacked. It was essential that the French government drive the development of the securitization market, and it did, largely because of its concern over the capital adequacy of its banks. The French government was a major shareholder in many banks, so it had a vested interest in their viability. Legislation permitting the issuance of securitized assets was passed in 1988, and the first issue reached the market in 1989. It was collateralized by auto loans, and the credit enhancement technique employed was the senior-subordinated structure. Why that technique was selected over third-party insurance company enhancement is illustrative of the role local laws and regulations play in the securitization field. Unlike accounting rules in the rest of the world, those in France in 1989 permitted banks to get off-balance-sheet treatment for the senior pieces they sold, even if they continued to hold the subordinated pieces containing the full risk of the issuance. The risk banks were supposed to be transferring through the sale was staying at home, but not in the eyes of the French regulators. This interpretation did not make sense and was changed at the end of 1993. This should help the market grow (see table 12.7).

The hand of the government was also evident in the requirement that mortgage-backed securities issues had to be authorized by and all transactions approved by the Commission des Opérations de Bourse (COB), the French equivalent of the Securities and Exchange Commission. No such requirement exists in the United Kingdom or United States. Thus, the market was more like a government enterprise.

Historic performance statistics on mortgage loans in France were woefully inadequate, so it was very difficult to predict what cash flows were going to be. This lack of data prohibited the structuring of long-term tranches, so the first transactions involved only short-term assets. The investors have been primarily domestic French institutions, a marked contrast from the broad investor group attracted to the U.K. mortgage deals. To date, the volume of product securitized in France has totaled $8 billion. Few of these issues were sold outside France because the spread was too thin for international investors who had to take a currency risk, as well as a credit and interest-rate risk.

For future issuance the outlook is uncertain. The need to gain regulatory approval, as well as market acceptance of securitized deals, will

Table 12.7
The French experience

- Government-driven initiative arising from concerns over bank capital adequacy

- 1988—Enabling legislation passed

- First issue, December 1989

- Senior/subordinated structures—favorable off-balance sheet treatment eliminated in 1993

- Commission des Opérations de Bourse regulation and approval of transactions

- Limited performance statistics

- Volume since first deal—only $8 billion—investors primarily domestic French institutions

---

slow development. In fast-paced world capital markets this is a serious limitation. The French, if they wish to expand securitization, would be well advised to study the flexible market approach to adapting structures to changing market conditions that has characterized the development of these markets in both the United States and the United Kingdom.

Toward Global Securitization

Table 12.8 presents a snapshot of the current status of securitization globally. There is a huge difference between the size of the markets in the United States and the size of those in other nations. Issuances of $500 million in Canada, the United Kingdom, France, Australia, and the rest of the world compare with issuances of $500 billion a year in U.S. securitized capital markets. The difference is huge. Big markets have the wherewithal to attract and afford the resources needed to do the job better. The developed market outside the United States, which would include the four nations mentioned earlier, has not yet reached a stage where it is creating a great deal of international excitement. Domestically, securitization can serve a purpose and, through competition, make local funding markets more efficient. Work should go forward on the basis of developing the building blocks necessary to grow securitization—standardization of applicable laws, grading of risk via underwriting guidelines, a database of historic performance statistics, and computers to handle the complexity of the analysis.

Table 12.8
Global securitization status

- United States
    Huge issuance—$500 billion + per year
- Canada, United Kingdom, France, Australia
    Developed market status
    Regular issuance—$500 million + per year
- Argentina, Mexico, Brazil, Chile, Spain, Sweden, Italy, Japan, Hong Kong, Philippines, India
    Emerging market status
    Irregular issuance—$25–$500 million per year
- Finland, Belgium, Indonesia, Malaysia
    Pioneering, pending first transaction

Greater understanding that the concept of linking borrowers directly to national and world capital markets works best when it is market driven will help expand these markets and improve their contributions to both borrowers and investors.

The International Outlook

The growth of securitization internationally is inevitable. It is not going to be easy, however, because it is a free market concept that typically lacks a strong local constituency and government support. The established local financial institutions will typically fight against the introduction of securitized markets. If we had governmental or quasi-governmental agencies like Freddie Mac or Fannie Mae in foreign capital markets, a launching platform would be in place. They could set underwriting standards and provide some measure of credit enhancement and historic statistics. Unfortunately, few such agencies exist elsewhere. Early steps to develop standards in credit practices and legal loan documents are very much recommended to any nation seeking the benefits of securitization. Table 12.9 summarizes the key elements in the outlook for securitization globally.

The international expansion of securitization, unfortunately, is likely to be slow, much slower than I envisioned seven years ago. The going is tough in so many countries because legal changes must precede any market action. Political risk is large. The legal fees are heavy at start up and without sizeable volume can be prohibitive. Other up-front costs, like computer networks and research, militate against the small deal and small market. Growth, when it comes, is likely to occur country by country.

Table 12.9
International outlook

- Growth is inevitable but it will not be easy—no government support
- Changes in legal/regulatory environments will be slow
- Country specific development will result in smaller and less liquid markets
- Issuer demand (capital constraints and cost of capital) will drive development pace
- Multicurrency deals will improve liquidity but with increased currency risk
- Lead times and up-front costs (particularly legal fees) will need to be reduced to get deals done
- U.S. technology exported to all countries

The force most likely to expand securitization is financial crisis. If there is a shortage of money to fund desirable activities in a developed nation and the traditional issuers of loans cannot do the job, the prospects for securitization rise. Government indifference will vanish, and support will increase. This has been our experience in the United States, for example, with home loans as the thrift system atrophied, with low-rated auto companies, like Chrysler, and most recently with commercial real estate. In emerging markets, the strong need to fund housing can potentially be met by the capital markets through securitization. Cross-border securitization with strong collateral and issuers is already being done. A case can be made for securitization to develop faster in the emerging markets because of the magnitude of the pressing basic needs and the lack of viable institutional intermediary systems.

I want to make one final point: It is clear that the expansion of securitization globally will be based on the concepts and the technology developed in the U.S. capital markets. These structures and techniques are wearing well and providing the measure of investor protection and performance promised. Our experience in the United Kingdom in the best of times and the worst of times is a powerful case in point. The task now is for bright and enterprising investment minds who understand the basic workings of our markets to become missionaries to the world—at a profit, of course.

13

A Case Study in International Securitization: Meeting the Needs of Developing Nations

Robert D. Graffam

The International Finance Corporation (IFC) is the world's largest provider of finance to private-sector entities in the developing world. It is related to, but not part of, the World Bank. Four agencies make up the World Bank Group. The World Bank, whose official name is the International Bank for Reconstruction and Development, was established in 1945. It lends to governments. The IFC was created eleven years later, in 1956, with the sole purpose of providing finance to the private sector. The other two agencies are the International Development Association, established in 1960, and the Multilateral Investment Guarantee Agency, established in 1988.

The IFC's mandate is to foster the development of the private sector through three specific activities. The first is an investment role; making loans and equity investments. The second is a mobilization role. In addition to funding, it gets other entities to colend, to join in funding projects. Typically, it raises six to seven dollars from colenders for each dollar that IFC invests. The third role is to provide financial advice.

Who owns the IFC? Basically, all the countries of the world. It is owned by 163 members, and the number is rising as countries split up and take on new configurations. Voting is weighted, and the larger countries can block initiatives that require supermajorities. The United States is the largest shareholder, with 24 percent of the votes. Table 13.1 lists our financial vital statistics as of December 1994, which show a total asset base in excess of $10 billion. Our strong capital base, a net worth of over 30 percent of total assets, provides us with a triple-A rating and enables us to fund ourselves almost entirely through the capital markets. The countries of the world provide the capital, and the agency leverages that by borrowing. In 1993, borrowings were $1.3 billion and in 1994, they will exceed $2.0 billion.

Table 13.1
IFC's financial strength, December 31, 1994

• Authorized capital	$2.45 billion
• Net worth	$3.41 billion
• Total assets	$10.5 billion
• Credit rating	AAA

Is the IFC a do-good organization or does it seek to turn a profit? It strives to do both. Over the past five or six years, however, one point has become clear. It cannot be developmental unless it is profitable. Profit must come first, and the agency must be able to stand the test of the market place. It has been profitable every year since inception and does operate on a commercial basis. Since its mandate requires IFC to operate in all parts of the world, some of which are not all that profitable, its return on equity objective is between 8 and 10 percent rather than the market's 15 to 20 percent. Some may describe this goal as self-sufficiency or self-sustaining rather than profit maximizing. Both its special status and goals make the promise and potential of securitization attractive to IFC. It can enable us to expand our reach without expanding our risk.

The International Finance Corporation participates only in private-sector ventures. It does not lend on the basis of government guarantees. It is a major provider of equity or risk capital in developing nations. In its role as a provider of venture capital, it follows market pricing policies. Lending rates are not government determined. As a point of reference, this year loans were priced at an average spread of three hundred basis points over the LIBOR rate. The presence of the IFC in a local market can be reassuring to other investors, particularly foreign investors (see table 13.2). A foreign investor entering a joint venture in a potentially hostile environment will welcome the IFC as a neutral party between the local partner and itself. Our role is often that of the neutral honest broker. We lessen political risk.

The Current Status of Securitization in the Developing World

Securitization is destined to play a growing role in international finance. Historically, it has done well in markets where there are a shortage of funds, deficiencies in credit quality despite a growing

Table 13.2
IFC's development role

- IFC presence reassures
  - Foreign investors
  - Local partners
  - Governments
- Honest broker/neutral partner
- Measure of political risk cover
- Catalyst for other investors and lenders

---

capacity to service debt, and a measure of uniformity in loan underwriting standards. Developing nations tend to meet the first two of these requirements. They also present the special challenge of currency risk and transfer risk as one moves funds from one currency and one nation to another. Given this latter risk, it seems appropriate that the early securitizations were cross-border transactions designed to keep currency risk neutral. Table 13.3 lists major transactions during the past three years. The lead advisor in every case was an American bank or investment banker. These transactions had several very distinctive features: In all instances they insulated the investor from country risk. The collateral assets happened to be originated in the developing nation, but the obligor was a major and known credit in the developed world. Many of the risk assets were telephone receivables where AT&T or MCI owed the money to the pool trustee. The transactions were designed so that the securitized structure captured the money before it went back to Mexico. There was no Mexican risk. You could say that AT&T owed the money. These transactions were private placements. None were done in the public market; none have been rated; no deals have been done where the investor is exposed to country risk.

The transactions described above in fact are not true securitizations. They are one-shot transactions that convert debt to security form and create potential liquidity and other values for investors. They do not, however, take standardized debt instruments, pool them, and convert the debt into unique securities transferring modified cash flows and new rights, privileges, and risks to the buyers. Neither did they involve bifurcation of cash flows or debt classes. In international finance, the term *securitization* is sometimes used inappropriately to describe transactions that are merely the conversion of bank debt into securities.

Table 13.3
Cross-border securitized transactions undertaken in Latin America

Country	Issuer	Amount (US$ million)	Tenor (yrs.)	Lead Advisor	Description
Mexico	Telmex (various tranches)	1,500	5	Citicorp	National telephone company. Telephone receivables purchase.
	Banamex	130	3	Citicorp	Largest Mexican bank. Credit card receivables purchase.
	Bancomer	230	5	Citicorp	Second largest Mexican bank. Credit card receivables purchase.
	CFE	235	5	Salomon Brothers	Electricity generating company. Electricity sale receivables purchase.
Argentina	Entel	24	5	Citicorp	National telephone company. Telephone receivables purchase.
Jamaica	Jamintel	73	10	Citicorp	National telephone company. Telephone receivables purchase.
Brazil	Embratel	70	10	Morgan	National telephone company. Telephone receivables purchase.
Honduras	Hondutel	11	5	Citicorp	Telephone receivables purchase.
Costa Rica	ICE	17	5	Citicorp	Telephone receivables purchase.
Venezuela	Sivensa	60	5.5	Citicorp	Large steel producer. Steel export receivables purchase.
Total		2,350			

The Brady bonds fall into that category. Most funds that have moved to developing countries through bond markets rather than through bank loans during the past few years do not qualify as securitizations.

The evolving nature of securitization in emerging markets is illustrated by the following Mexican transaction. In 1992, Kidder Peabody brought to market two deals for Nacional Financiera S.A. (NAFIN), a very large development bank that lends to commercial banks throughout Mexico. This structured transaction involved creating a Mexican trust that pooled the loans NAFIN had purchased from banks and selling interests internationally in this floating-rate issue. Recapping the deal, we had a very large, apex financial institution in Mexico which lends to banks. It bought loans from eighteen banks and put them into a special purpose Mexican trust and sold interests in that trust as floating-rate notes around the world. The issue is guaranteed by NAFIN. One may ask, what is the purpose of creating the new structure if in fact the deal is sold on the strength of the NAFIN guarantee? This is simply another issue of a known and respected issuer.

The second time around, however, changes were made. A year later, in 1993, NAFIN was able to remove its guarantee. The securitized issue stood on its own. Duff and Phelps rated the second issue triple-B, investment grade.[1] Now, you had a legitimate securitization. Mexican banks sold loan receivables into a trust that issued floating-rate notes in international markets on the credit of the notes and appropriate enhancements. The spreads on both transactions, interestingly, were almost the same. The first issue traded at 250 basis points over LIBOR; the second, at 245 basis points over LIBOR. We are beginning to see more such transactions, and they are more typical of classic securitizations.

Why are cross-border securitizations so difficult? Figure 13.1 sets forth the two challenges confronting anyone seeking to structure a securitized product for international markets. They are default risk, which requires the structure to be able to handle equity stress, and transfer risk, which requires the structure to be able to withstand liquidity stress. To meet liquidity stress and equity stress, the level of credit enhancement must necessarily be greater because of a lack of standardized underwriting guidelines, a lack of historic statistics on the performance of risks over cycles, and uncertainty regarding legal risks. Rating agencies are both knowledgeable and cautious. When in doubt, especially if the issuer is pioneering new products and concepts, the agency is likely to hold credit enhancement levels very high. If a first-time deal blows up, their credibility is jeopardized. It is the second challenge, however, the transfer risk, which makes cross-border financing different. This special risk flows from the fact that all the

---

1. These bonds were probably downgraded recently as a result of the well-publicized collapse of the Mexican peso and the consequent downgrading of Mexican sovereign debt by all major rating agencies.

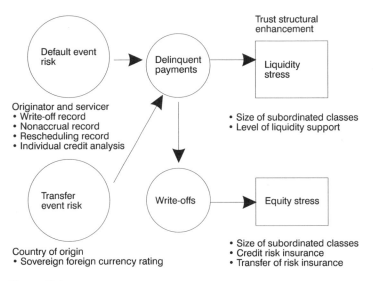

Figure 13.1
Risk elements in LDC assets

cash flow payments must go through a specific central bank. What happens if the payment flow gets interrupted? How do you factor in this event risk? Rating agencies use what is called the weakest-link theory in evaluating the worst-case risk and assigning ratings. The sovereign credit ratings of most developing nations are quite low, at most double-B+ and triple-B on the Standard & Poor's scale, and this can become the weakest link. In the case of a transaction that involves cross-border flows through a developing country, the rating of that nation can become the highest rating an issue can achieve. It is an uphill fight.

The Potential for Securitization in the Developing World

Cross-border securitizations of receivables are likely to increase for several reasons. First, there will continue to be transactions, such as the long-distance telephone credits, where the transfer risk is eliminated from consideration. Cash flows can be captured in the developed world. Second, the world has become very yield conscious and, as in the NAFIN transactions, will accept a proven private aggregator's paper. Emerging market assets, well selected and priced at 250 basis points over LIBOR, generate interest and enthusiasm. In essence investors are saying, "OK, we are not trying to get rid of the Mexican risk. We accept the risk; just pay us for it." Recent events in Mexico have interrupted capital flows to emerging markets but have not changed this premise; at the end of the day they will simply increase the price at which foreign investors are prepared to take emerging market risk.

Will the emerging market volume of securitized international transactions grow to a healthy level and become a sustainable source of financing for developing nations? I very much doubt it. The interest today appears to be opportunistic. On the issuer side, it may be difficult to assemble continuously the volume of qualified assets to pool. The lack of standardized documentation, historical data on defaults and foreclosures, and issues of civil law and transfer risk all work against homogeneity and fluidity. The more sophisticated applications of securitization techniques seem inapplicable at the present time. More important, on the investor side, it may be even more difficult to assemble a large universe of international investors willing to accept a homogeneous, standardized structure of pooled assets.

A second potential application of securitization techniques in developing nations is within the local markets themselves. What are the prospects for creating domestic markets similar to those developed over the past decade in the United States for home loans and other asset-backed products? To date, the level of domestic securitizations has been minimal. Very modest programs were instituted in Trinidad and Tobago by the IFC and by the government in Malaysia. Marcia Myerberg (see chapter 12) has noted the beginnings of activity in six or seven other emerging nations. The total in dollars, however, remains small.

Housing finance is the area where the needs are the greatest and the performance has been the poorest. In Eastern Europe and the former Soviet Republics, countries striving to make the transition from a centrally planned economy to a market economy, housing and housing finance was provided by the state. Now it must be provided privately. Financial intermediaries dedicated to housing finance do not exist. Government guarantors, like Ginnie Mae, Fannie Mae, and Freddie Mac, do not exist. Thus, to encourage home ownership, new forms of housing finance are extremely important. Securitization can be important to meeting the housing needs of emerging nations.

In some nations, the concept of a mortgage does not exist; in others there is no way to enforce repossessions. The concept of a trust may have no basis in law. The American securitization paradigm does not flow automatically to new nations. The concept is at best adapted to new nations by trial and error.

An Asian Experiment

The experience of the International Finance Corporation in Indonesia is an interesting case in point. Table 13.4 outlines an effort by the IFC and others to introduce securitization concepts into Indonesia. The nation has no agencies like Freddie Mac, or Fannie Mae, or rated credit enhancers, nor even the legal basis permitting an issuer to create a trust. IFC is working with P. T. Citimas Capital, Indonesia to create a privately owned financial insurance company not only to provide financial guarantees but also to originate, structure, and enhance asset-backed securities. The goal is to create securitized product for the domestic market, and we will go so far as to originate loans to our own standards to do so. In a sense this will parallel what Salomon did when it took the securitization concept to the United Kingdom. The entities that came together in P. T. Citimas are Capital Markets Assurance Corporation (CapMAC), a privately owned monoline financial insurance company in the United States with a 15 percent interest, the IFC with a 15 percent interest, and Citibank. Two Indonesian groups

Table 13.4
IFC's proposed investment in P. T. Citimas Capital Indonesia

Concept	Create a local, privately owned financial insurance company that would provide structuring, credit enhancement, and placement services for pools of domestic assets including mortgages, and consumer finance receivables.
Shareholders/Sponsors	- Capital Markets Assurance Corporation (CapMAC-technical partner)
	- Citibank (will provide initial asset origination)
	- Two Indonesian groups
	- IFC
Capitalization	Rp 15 billion (US $2.1 million)
Credit Enhancement	To take usual form-over-collateralization, partial guarantees from company, subordinated tranches, etc.
Problems	No trust law in Indonesia. No possibility of creating special purpose vehicles. The company will have to take assets onto its own balance sheet and fund them through "limited recourse" bonds. Limited institutional investor market.

will be the majority owners. CapMAC will provide the technical assistance, and Citibank will originate a good deal of the loans to be securitized. The IFC will play its usual honest-broker role between the foreign and local partners.

Because of the lack of trust law in Indonesia, as well as the impossibility of creating special purpose vehicles, the company will have to take the asset pools onto its own balance sheet and fund them through "limited recourse" bonds. Such a structure has limits to its potential because it is capital consumptive. The Indonesian authorities, given their rapidly growing economy, are very desirous of expanding markets for consumer durables, and legal and regulatory innovation is likely. One of the positive aspects of introducing new financing techniques into emerging markets is that you can get a fresh start. Starting out in a vacuum, you do not have to repeal old laws. And often, you can get a commitment from government to develop the necessary regulatory framework relatively quickly.

Will the Indonesian experiment work? The positive factors are a growth economy, committed sponsors with a profit motive, and committed governmental authorities all seeking to launch, adapt, and grow the concept. The negatives are the lack of a regulatory/legal framework; lack of appropriate securities market infrastructure, including the limited presence of institutional investors; and the lack of homogeneity in the practices of banks originating consumer loans.

If securitized markets can be developed to finance human needs, the potential is huge. Indonesia is a country of 180 million people. The market for housing finance is enormous. If a sustainable market—not a series of one-time transactions like those early cross-border securitizations—evolves, the new financing techniques can change the face of Indonesia and even its status in the world. It has not happened yet, and the problems to be overcome are formidable, but the effort has begun. Check in a few years, and see how far we have come.

Latin America and Asia Loan Trust

The International Finance Corporation is currently at work on a plan to securitize its own balance sheet. The IFC generates a large volume of floating-rate loans around the world denominated in U.S. dollars. The loans are essentially commercial contracts to private, not governmental, organizations. The composition of the first pool, Latin America and Asia Loan Trust 1994-A, at $400 million, is shown in figure 13.2

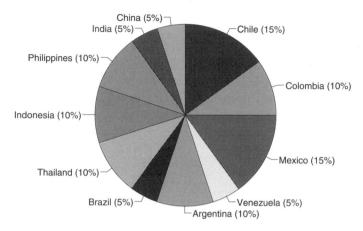

China (5%)
India (5%)
Chile (15%)
Philippines (10%)
Colombia (10%)
Indonesia (10%)
Mexico (15%)
Thailand (10%)
Brazil (5%)
Venezuela (5%)
Argentina (10%)

Figure 13.2
Latin America and Asia Loan Trust, 1994-A pool composition

and table 13.5. The $400 million pool contains seventy-five loans from eleven countries and twenty different economic sectors to give it diversification. The maximum exposure per loan is 2.5 percent and the average exposure per loan is 1.3 percent. The maximum exposure per country is 15 percent, the maximum exposure per sector is 11 percent, and the maximum exposure per sector/country is 5 percent. We also employed minimums in constructing the pool. Clearly, the Trust will not have the diversity of American mortgage or auto pools, with their thousands of obligors, but for a commercial and industrial loan trust it has reasonable diversification.

Table 13.5 provides further information on the characteristics of the loans in the Trust. Rates on average are 180 basis points over LIBOR, in part because many of the loans are well seasoned.

The IFC is planning to use a senior subordinated structure in its Off-Shore Trust. As shown graphically in figure 13.3, there are three tranches or classes. The senior receivables, having first claim on all cash flows, should be able to earn a double-A and possibly a triple-A rating. This is by far the largest class, and the size of this class is critical to the profitability of the transaction to the IFC. The intermediate, or B class, should also be investment grade and priced at a yield attractive to the market. The class C securities, or residuals, will be retained by IFC. The deal also includes two additional features to handle cash flow timing problems. The Interest Rate Basis Swap, shown at the top of figure 13.3, represents a relatively small and technical cash flow. The Trust will purchase floating-rate loans originated by IFC and will fund

Table 13.5
Latin America and Asia Loan Trust 1994-A

Country	Loans	$ million	% of Pool	Spread (bps)
Argentina	11	40.00	10.00	230.00
Brazil	10	20.00	5.00	176.25
Chile	4	60.00	15.00	191.67
Colombia	7	40.00	10.00	159.38
Mexico	11	60.00	15.00	178.75
Venezuela	2	20.00	5.00	175.00
Latin America	45	240.00	60.00	186.77
China	3	20.00	5.00	165.00
India	6	20.00	5.00	161.88
Indonesia	10	40.00	10.00	205.00
Philippines	5	40.00	10.00	200.00
Thailand	6	40.00	10.00	118.13
Asia	30	160.00	40.00	171.64
Total Pool	75	400.00	100.00	180.72

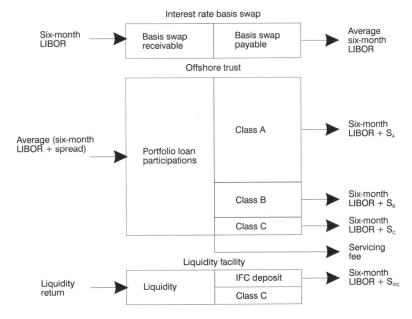

Figure 13.3
Overall structure of transaction

them by issuing floating-rate certificates. However, the LIBOR reset date on the two sides of a transaction might be different. The certificates will reset on two days in the year, say January 15 and July 15, but the seventy-five individual loans can reset at various dates during the year. The Interest Rate Basis Swap covers that risk. We would be receiving LIBOR that resets throughout the year and paying LIBOR with two definite reset dates.

The Liquidity Facility shown at the bottom of figure 13.3 will provide cash to make up for shortfalls in payments due to delays in getting funds on time from eleven countries and through the various central banks. The transaction in effect will handle its own liquidity stress.

As for liquidity risk, the IFC, unlike foreign commercial banks lending in countries, has never experienced a transfer event in which a country has involuntarily rescheduled payments to it. The agency has preferential access to the foreign exchange of countries, albeit not always on a punctual basis. During the height of the debt crisis of the mid-1980s there were some payment delays in excess of sixty days, but the arrears were cleared up reasonably quickly. There are big differences in the ways governments behave when they cannot pay their debts. They may treat private banks summarily, but not the IFC. In a sense, our position is not dissimilar to that of Freddie Mac or Fannie Mae in the home loan markets. You do not renege on agency contracts because you know you are going to need them in the future. We are viewed as a most favored lender. My challenge in negotiating our rating with the credit agencies is to get credit for that special status from them.

The goal in constructing the pool was to avoid concentrations of systemic risks, where an entire class might be exposed to the same worldwide forces at the same time. First, we assured that no loan category in any country accounted for more than 5 percent of the aggregate risk of the pool. The biggest exposure using that filter was in the printing, publishing, and broadcasting industry in Chile at 5 percent. Second, there was historic evidence that there can be a high correlation of losses in Latin American countries during a debt crisis. So, this exposure had to be limited. Is there a correlation between the defaults of Mexico and China? There is probably not, and the rating agencies agree. As for industry groupings, some commodity sectors, like oil, gold, and other extractive industries, play to world market forces and represent correlated risk. However, loans to textile plants

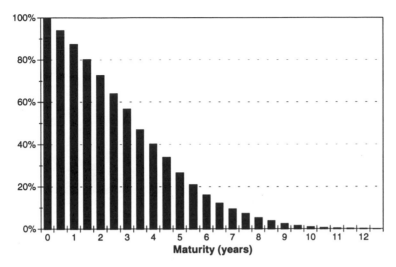

Figure 13.4
Pool principal outstanding (as % of initial principal)

in Argentina, China, and Poland are unlikely to represent any common exposure. Banking is another industry where risks do not seem to be correlated. So, by creating a matrix and analyzing risks, we strive to construct pools that provide a measure of internal diversification. This gives rating agencies and investors significant comfort that timely payment of interest and ultimate payment of principal can and will be made.

To reduce pressures on borrowers, the typical IFC 10-year loan calls for semiannual interest only for the first three years and then interest and principal during years four through ten. The average life of our loans is between five and six years. Figures 13.4, 13.5, and 13.6 show the historic performance of IFC loans. The record has been a very good one, and through structuring we believe performance will be enhanced. The pool principal pays down relatively quickly with a half-life of just under four years (see figure 13.4). Nonaccruing loans, those over sixty days past due, vary significantly by year, with a peak between 14 and 18 percent during the years of the foreign debt crisis, 1985 to 1987 (see figure 13.5). Note that the loans sixty days in arrears for our pool countries were significantly lower than arrears on all loans. Most delinquencies cure. We do workouts and reschedulings. On project financing, if there is a shock to the project, restructuring and rescheduling become a first order of business. By the end of the

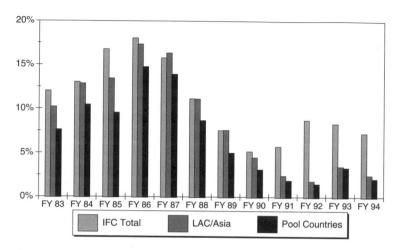

Figure 13.5
Loans in nonaccrual status (as % of loans principal outstanding). According to IFC's criteria a loan is classified in "nonaccrual" status if interest or principal payments are at least sixty days overdue.

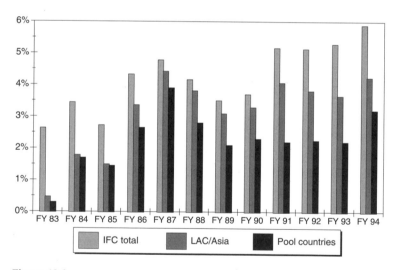

Figure 13.6
Cumulative net write-offs (as % of cumulative principal closed-out loans)

debt crisis, perhaps 20 to 25 percent of our loans were rescheduled or recycled. Since the loans are floating rate, not fixed-rate product, investors are a great deal more accommodating to extensions of maturities. As a consequence, IFC's net write-offs in the pool countries have

Table 13.6
Transfer risk definition and effects

- Transfer risk, also known as "currency convertibility risk" or "foreign exchange impairment risk" is defined as the probability that borrowers facing the obligation to make a payment in foreign currency might not be able to convert their own domestic currency cash flow into the required foreign exchange in a timely fashion.

- Transfer risk differs from commercial risk (where borrowers do not have sufficient funds to service their obligations) in that sufficient funds are available but borrowers are not able to convert them into the foreign currency in which the obligations are denominated.

- A transfer risk event (for a given class of creditors) is defined as the inability of all borrowers in one country to service foreign currency obligations due to the central bank's inability or unwillingness to convert domestic currency into foreign currency in order to service the obligations. It is possible that a transfer risk event in a country may selectively affect a certain class of creditors while not affecting others.

- The effect of a transfer risk event is a delay in the cash flows due during the duration of the event from all the loan participations in that country.

- The main characteristics of a transfer risk event, as experienced by supranational institutions, are: (1) it is transient, with a duration that depends on the severity of the event; (2) it affects all the loans in a given country; (3) it delays all interest and principal payments due during the duration of the event; and (4) the delayed cash flows (plus accrued interest) are fully recovered at the end of the event.

---

averaged around 2.5 percent over the past decade (see figure 13.6). If the average life of a loan is around five plus years, this means that the annual write-off would average .5 percent per year. Our history on losses, by the way, goes back to 1956 and includes the years of the major debt crisis in less developed countries. These write-offs are very much below those of the American commercial banks on foreign loans.

In creating an international securitization, the final element is sovereign risk, or transfer risk, and it weighs heavily on the transaction. This is the risk that an investor across a border will not receive timely payments because the borrower, even though able and willing, cannot send funds out of the country due to central bank or government interference. Understanding and selling this risk is one of the biggest hurdles in negotiating your rating with the rating agencies, Standard and Poor's, Moody's, and others.

Table 13.6 defines transfer risk and discusses its potential effects on investors. In our pool, most of the countries were rated double-B and double-B+. Standard and Poor's, under its weakest-link theory, says that the weakest link in a deal will determine its rating—in this case the exposure to a double-B nation. And, we were seeking a double-A or triple-A rating on the issue. We had to convince that agency that default manifests itself very differently when the cause is sovereign risk and not credit default risk. If the borrower does not pay, very likely a write-off is in prospect. If the sovereign does not have sufficient foreign exchange and transfer risk hits, it is a liquidity crisis, not an equity crisis. The trust structure can be designed to handle liquidity stress so that investors continue to receive timely payments and thereby warrant a top rating. It is to be hoped the rating agencies will come to that conclusion.

If this is so, then, the Latin America and Asia Loan Trust 1994-A will come to the market as a senior subordinate offering with between 80 percent and 85 percent of the total receivables in class A, rated double-A or better, 10 to 15 percent in class B, which will be unrated, and 5 percent in class C.

From a purely financial point of view, does it make sense for the IFC to do this transaction? It will take the first losses on the class C tranche and on the liquidity facility. That is the extent of the enhancement it is offering investors. And, the breakeven here is a spread of fifty basis points a year. Given an average life of four years, if the cumulative write-offs do not exceed 2 percent during the life of the pool, we will break even in terms of the C tranche. If cumulative defaults are less, we make money. If they are higher, we lose money. Obviously, if we are able to issue a higher percentage in class A securities, or if our assumptions regarding spreads are too generous, our break-even point will change.

Right now the deal is marginally profitable. As a pilot project, it offers exciting potential. The opportunity for the IFC to use its triple-A balance sheet to raise funds for private-sector development in emerging markets will be a breakthrough. The key will be market acceptance of the structure and investor comfort with how we handle transfer risk.

The strong interest of the International Finance Corporation in securitization flows from our pursuit of several corporate goals. As a triple-A-rated agency with a very strong balance sheet, we would like to become totally self-sustaining and not have to go back to our shareholder nations for additional capital in the future. If we can generate sufficient returns on continuing operations, this will be possible. Securitization is a mechanism for balance sheet management that can enable us to do that. It can enable us to attract major institutional investors internationally to provide funds to developing nations on a safe and diversified basis. In the past, banks were the primary private credit conduit of funds from developed to emerging nations. Through the structuring of risk and appropriate guarantees we may very well be able to be the catalyst that brings the cutting edge of first world finance to new areas of great need. The history of securitization indicates that when funds vacuums exist, securitization is able to make its greatest strides.

14 The Risks, Potential, and Promise of Securitization

Lowell Bryan

This essay discusses securitization and its place in the financial economy. In particular, what does securitization mean for the alternative ways of distributing and intermediating credit products?

The essential banking business system was invented in the Middle Ages. It has had a long life cycle, some five or six hundred years, and it basically has not changed much since it was invented. The system relies on the law of large numbers, which means that at no one time will all depositors want their money. As long as a bank has adequate capital so that depositors have confidence in the bank and there is no bank panic, a bank will have a stable base of deposits that can be loaned out at a price that is higher than what depositors are paid. One big pool of capital absorbs all of the risk. Another characteristic of the banking system is that the banker does not care where the net interest margin comes from, that is, which customers pay it. Bankers just want to know that there is enough interest and fees net of operating expense to cover the cost of their capital. The operating costs are largely shared across the entire customer base. However, this business system is becoming obsolete. Given the technologies available today, this is a relatively crude method of intermediation. It relies on the intermediary maintaining the capital to absorb the aggregate risk of all of the borrowers from the bank. But individual borrowers represent very different risks, and the amount of capital needed to absorb credit risk varies dramatically with the borrower. On the liability side, this system relies on underpaying for deposits relative to the economic value of those deposits in the money markets.

Not so long ago in this country, there was a series of local banking oligopolies throughout the nation. These oligopolies were still in place when I entered the banking system, in 1969. It was a comfortable world for bankers. Then came major changes for the industry, securitization being one of the principal ones, globalization of funds being another. The industry went from a stable oligopoly, under which the banking system had a monopoly on the liquid assets of the nation, to one where funds were raised through money market mutual funds and then invested in money market instruments, commercial paper, and so forth. The whole process of what we then called disintermediation and what is now called securitization began, and the banking industry lost its control of the nation's liquidity.

By the early 1980s competition in the banking industry had really intensified. The financial industry began to see market share shifts and competition to extend credit. This competition for credit business was not confined just to price but extended to terms and conditions. Over time, the industry structure began to be shaped by competition. The only way acquisitions could be made, because of the Bank Holding Company Act, was through friendly takeovers. Hostile takeovers could not be made. Major differences in skills began to be observed as some of the better banks began to take larger market shares. The banks that could not keep up, as they lost their best deposits and assets to securitization, began to take risks aggressively in order to maintain their net interest margin.

The traditional banking business system discussed earlier depends on maintaining a stable net interest margin. In the late 1980s, a lot of those aggressive risks became losses. Many banks were taken over by stronger banks; essentially, the thrift industry disappeared, and we entered into a discontinuity that has many years still to run. We saw massive market share shifts and saw widening margins after the intense price-competitive era of the late 1980s. The whole industry structure is in flux. The winners are consolidating a real payoff for skills built up in the 1980s, and we are seeing a retreat from aggressive, or uneconomic, risk taking. At some stage out there, after the year 2000, we will probably get to a new competitive equilibrium, even though the closer we get to the year 2000, the further out that new competitive equilibrium seems to be. It seems as if this discontinuity has a long time to run.

I will discuss several major trends, only one of which is securitization. It is easy to think of securitization in a vacuum, as a trend by itself. In fact it, in combination with a whole series of other trends, is reshaping the world's financial systems, the world's way of intermediating funds. The forces at work include technology, the elimination of geographic and product barriers, securitization, globalization, and demographic changes. There are both hard technology, such as tele-communications changes, computers, software and analytics, and soft technology, such as structured securitized credit, for example, deriva-tive instruments. These changes in the techniques of production are in fact the driving force behind everything. The banking business system that was invented in the mid-1500s is on the last legs of an S-curve of a product life cycle. The whole bundle of technology called banking is a very mature technology and is being displaced by a different one based upon securities, which is still in a rapid growth phase.

One may ask what these other trends have to do with securitization. Within a few years, banking with nonbranch distribution is going to have a big impact. Distribution will be through all sorts of multimedia, perhaps interactive personal computers, smart phones, interactive tele-visions, or something else. All of these forms have one thing in com-mon. They remove the need to be physically local. You will be able to create national credit intermediaries, for example, that will be able to standardize terms and conditions for small business loans across the nation. They will be able to look customers in the eye without being physically located near the customer. As these pools of assets with standardized terms are created they will be able to be securitized and distributed nationally or even globally. This is just a small example of what the new forces can mean to banks and to nonbank financial intermediaries. Our clients are just beginning to look at what this one set of technologies means to the way they operate. In the longer term, as it removes the need for physical presence, it will erode one of the last bastions of the traditional banking business system.

Service after service is being taken national and is being pursued on a disaggregated basis by national players. This is enabled by technol-ogy. Both the credit card and the ATM industries are in a mature phase in which the local banks are playing only limited roles. This process is taking place in many products; for example, we believe that the checking system, which is the core of banking, will eventually wind up in the hands of national utilities. The payment monopoly that the industry has had will be owned by a few banks, but also by some nonbanks as well. On the regulatory front, we are close to getting rid of some of the regulatory barriers that have prevented the banking industry from being truly national. By the year 2000, if not in the next year or two, national branching, we believe, will be a reality. Finally, we believe product barriers separating banking, securities, and insur-ance will all fall in the next few years. In a few short years it will no longer be sensible to look at financial services as a series of industries defined by their regulatory features. These changes all should have taken place ten years ago. They are now likely to take place, with a high degree of probability, within the next five years. Soon, you will not be talking about a separate life insurance industry, or a property and casualty industry, or a retail security industry. It is harder to talk about them right now as separate industries rather than as a personal financial services industry.

Let us, though, concentrate on securitization for a minute. Securities have a lot of advantages over loans. The driving force behind securitization is that it is simply more cost effective. The cost of an intermediation system based upon the securitization processes is less than 50 basis points for most financial product lines. If you look at mutual funds going to commercial paper, the cost of the system is much less than even 50 basis points. By contrast, banks require nearly 400 or 500 basis points of net interest margin to operate their business system. It cannot be done for less than 200 basis points because that is the cost of equity capital, plus the regulatory costs, plus irreducible operating expenses. Simply said, you have at least 150 basis points to play with for any asset class if you are competing against a bank. If you can figure out some way to securitize the asset (i.e., avoid the bank's capital costs and regulatory costs), you can pocket the difference. Over time, the number of classes of assets that were viewed to be impossible to securitize have gone down and down. Clever people have found ever more innovative ways to leverage the cost advantages of securities over bank intermediation to securitize more and more assets.

When I talk about securitization, I am not just talking about structured securitized credit. I am including all forms of raising money through securities, including the direct issuance of debt by governments. In fact, the single most important form of securitization going on right now is just plain old direct issuances of government debt. Then comes the direct issuance of debt by corporations, money market mutual funds, bond funds, and REITs (Real estate investment trusts). In addition, of course, there is structured securitized debt such as the mortgage-backed securities, the traded receivable pools, and the traded loans.

Increasingly, you are finding the trends not only in the United States, but in country after country, albeit with about a 10-year lag behind the U.S. system. If you look at commercial paper penetration as a percentage of GNP, most developed nations outside of the United States are roughly where the United States was about ten years ago. How fast securitization proceeds in any particular country has a lot to do with whether or not the local banking system and the central banks embrace it. Even if they do not embrace it, over time, the economic cost of competing against securitization is causing more and more entities in each country to begin to consider it. McKinsey is working with a Canadian institution, and it is about to embrace securitization after having resisted it for a decade. All you need is one catalyst, one major institution in a country to embrace securitization, then all of a sudden the whole game starts.

The amount of assets that are traded, that is, securitized, is increasing. The amount of illiquid assets that do not move off the balance sheets is decreasing as a part of the flow of funds. About three or four years ago I argued that there were some classes of assets that could not be securitized. I was referring to small business loans, middle-market loans, commercial real estate loans, and developing country debt. All of these have now been securitized. There will still be some assets that will not be securitized, namely, those in which the risk is lumpy and the market volumes are too small to make it worthwhile. Having said that, I think these assets will be a small fraction of the total assets in the flow of funds.

One of the implications of securitization for banks and securities firms is that there will be a large number of suppliers who are going to be competing for a dwindling supply of credit. If you persist in the old business system, there will not be much out there going forward. Value is migrating toward those people who originate the loans, credit underwrite the loans, or credit structure the loans and is migrating away from those who bear the credit risk. The reason banks are still around is because of the other side of the balance sheet, the deposit side. If you have deposits, you must have assets. If they are not loans, they will be securities. So, increasingly, the asset side of the balance sheet will be filled up with securities. When you do that, of course, it means that you must earn your money from the deposit side. The reason why banks are paying only 1 or 2 percent for demand deposits is because depositors are now paying the full cost of the deposits. Banks are no longer able to make the spread from the lending side, and so they must make it all from the deposit and payment side. That is why checking and other fees are going up too.

Credit risk is moving to the securities market. One of the historic barriers to securitization was that the securities market was reluctant to take real credit risk. Increasingly, the securities market is willing to take real credit risk. It used to be hard to push triple-B paper. Now, the high-yield market is buoyant again even after its collapse just a few years ago. When you put all this together, the long-term role of banking as a business is being brought into question. However, as I will discuss later, I think that banks will still exist; they are just going to look a lot different.

Although there is a major increase in demand for securities services, it is important to remember that a large proportion of the value added of securitization relative to banking is captured by the end users—the investors and the borrowers. At the end of the day, the mortgage-backed securities system has probably knocked at least one full percentage point off the cost of mortgages. This is income that has been taken away from intermediaries and has basically gone to the borrowers.

Finally, consider how globalization is changing banking. Until about 1973, when Bretton Woods broke down, the only capital flowing between nations was to finance trade flows. There was no global capital market; only national capital markets. Therefore, the only way that national economies interacted was through trade. This system broke down and is now long obsolete. In the 1970s, once the global capital markets began to be freed, there was a shift from a series of national segregated markets to the beginnings of a global marketplace. What globalized first was money, foreign exchange. In the 1980s what globalized were bonds. In the 1990s what is globalizing are equities. Sometime in the next century we will have a fully integrated global capital market, one in which people base their decisions primarily on the direct returns on their investments, as opposed to worrying about currency risk and the other risks associated with international investment. We are not there yet, but we are headed in that direction. One of the most important forces driving the globalization of markets has been the proliferation of derivatives. People have found all sorts of ways to use derivatives to link formerly separate markets. In the mid-1970s investment bankers undertook transactions that involved borrowing money in one currency, lending in another currency, and covering the risk with a forward contract. At that time the spread might have been between 1 and 2 percent in some markets. Today, the spreads on this arbitrage are five or ten basis points, barely enough to cover the transaction costs. These costs have also fallen. Twenty years ago it may have cost five or ten thousand dollars to do such a transaction, counting the investment bankers' time and so forth. Now the cost is between ten and twenty dollars. All of these markets are now linked together.

What does this have to do with securitization? One of the major ways in which the global marketplace has grown is through securitization. Loans were taken out of banks, where they could not be traded, and were put into the market, where they could be traded, and therefore linked up. To give a perspective on how big this market is now, I can point out in 1980 the total financial stock of the developed world's financial system was $10 trillion, of which $5 trillion was essentially the money supply, that is, the banking system. That is what globalized first. Today the global financial system has roughly $35 trillion of assets, of which roughly $25 trillion is globalized. Conceptually, what is going on is that these markets are growing, first by geographic expansion—new countries are being added—then new instruments are being added, and finally, emerging countries are joining on top of it. Securitization is continually increasing the amount of assets within the intermediary system that can be linked together into the global marketplace. An overwhelmingly powerful global capital market is developing which begins to feed on itself. For example, if a nation with the traditional banking system tries to resist the trend, depositors will simply go into money market mutual funds in other countries. The ability to maintain a banking oligopoly is disappearing in country after country. The capital market is rewarding those countries that liberalize their financial systems and is penalizing the investors and depositors in those countries that are not.

To get a sense for how big this market is getting, McKinsey did research projecting forward, instrument by instrument, how big the global market was going to be. From today's financial stock of $35 trillion, the projected stock of financial assets by the year 2000 is on the order of $85 trillion. The relationship to GDP is going from twice to three times GDP. Remember, there is no reason why financial assets cannot grow faster than GDP, and they have. Once financial assets are out of the banking system you can have an infinite multiplier. There is no reserve requirement. You borrow, relend, borrow, relend and create financial assets as long as you have people on both sides of the balance sheet. In terms of exports, the stock of financial assets is thirteen times the size of all OECD (Organization for Economic Cooperation and Development) exports. By the year 2000, the ratio is projected to be twenty to one. We think that developing countries, which barely are part of this market now, will represent a significant share by the year 2000.

In terms of the different asset categories, in 1980, 45 percent of the financial stock was in banks, essentially the money supply. By the year 2000 this figure will be down to 20 percent. The other 80 percent of the financial stock will be outside the banking system in securities form of one kind or another. The class of assets that is growing the fastest is government bonds, up from 18 percent of a $10 trillion base to 35 percent of an $85 trillion base. That is what I referred to earlier—the biggest single cause of securitization is direct issuance of debt by governments. That was why Bretton Woods broke down. Governments did not want to be constrained by the rigidities of the Bretton Woods system, and they have been the biggest takers of funds from the global financial marketplace. Look at how much momentum this financial marketplace has and how little it is connected to the direct real economy, for example, to traded goods. Foreign exchange was twelve times export volume as recently as 1983. Foreign exchange is now forty-six times export volume. Clearly, most foreign exchange transactions have nothing to do with the exchange of traded goods. It has everything to do with the global capital marketplace.

Securitization and globalization work together. Securitization is the way assets get into the system so that they can be integrated into the global capital market. Throughout the world, trading volume continues to grow relative to real GDP growth. This means that, increasingly, interest rates and exchange rates are going to be determined globally rather than nationally. Exchange rates, interest rates, and securities prices will be volatile over the foreseeable future. A lot of the risk of being in the securities business, in fact, is derived from new linkages being forged in the global capital markets, so all of a sudden prices behave differently. Recent experience has made clear that what drives long-term bond rates is different than what it was in the past. As these linkages are formed, new techniques are developed, new players are involved, and prices begin to operate differently. All of the modeling, based upon history, all of a sudden goes up in smoke.

Increasingly, if you are going to play in this market, you need global capital market skills. It does not matter if you only have local customers, you must be part of the global capital market. There will be only a few institutions that can really play in this whole global capital market as broad-based, full-line global players. There will be hundreds of attractive niche roles, particularly in investment management. There will be a large value in using derivatives to serve customer needs. Increasingly, when you talk about securitization, you cannot talk about it separately from derivatives. A lot of value added, a lot of the way that you capture the profits is in the structuring of the transactions; you invariably use derivatives as a large part of the structuring.

One last trend influencing banking that is less obvious is demographics. Consider a very simple model of demographics. Assume there are only three kinds of people: young workers, mature workers, and retired workers. Young workers pay income and social security taxes and are net borrowers. Mature workers pay income and social security taxes and are net savers. Retired workers are net users of entitlements, have a propensity to shift their assets from property to financial assets, and form cohesive voting blocks. This is important because the mix of these is changing fairly rapidly.

In 1980, the United States had a huge set of people in the young worker category. The reason the United States was able to sustain such large deficits in the 1980s, at the same time that the population was in peak borrowing years, was that the global capital market took advantage of the savings generated by an increasingly elderly population in Japan and Germany. The United States imported capital, and the borrowing rates were lower than they otherwise would have been. If you project forward ten years, the U.S. baby boomers are now moving into the peak saving and financial accumulation years, as is the population of the rest of the industrial world. This trend keeps on until about the year 2020, and this is going to have a huge impact on the supply of funds. There will actually be a shortage of borrowers. The people that want to borrow are declining as a relative percentage of the population. There will be a large number of people who want high returns from saving and, other than the governments, a relatively small number of people in the developed world who want to borrow. The natural outcome of these demographics is that governments will borrow for consumption, which is probably not what most of us want to see.

Consider the relation between age and financial assets and liability accumulation. If you look at people between the ages of twenty-five and forty-four, they have significant net financial liabilities relative to assets. By the time they are forty-five to sixty, they are in balance. After sixty-five, they are significant net financial asset accumulators.

You not only have a shift in age, you also have a polarization of wealth. The polarization of wealth is coming about because the globalization of the real economy is breaking down oligopolies and the control of prices for end-products and labor. The value of pure labor is being reduced, and the value of skill and knowledge is increased in the global marketplace. The value of skill and knowledge is also being increased through technology. The mobility of capital is enabling smart people to understand the market and make a lot more money, too. In other words, the people with money are better able to earn higher returns. When you watch the statistics, wealth is becoming more concentrated. The top 10 percent of U.S. households own over 70 percent of the financial assets. Wealth in other countries tends to be even more concentrated.

This has important implications for banks. Banks have been geared toward the median, not the mean. Borrowers have been paying the freight for banks. As you go to investment management products, you have an infrastructure that does not fit the change in demographics of the population. Some of the implications of the demographic trends on banks and securities firms are that you have lessening demands for credit, greater needs to use securities to offset deposits, great demand for investment management services, great demand for private banking services, continual search for yield, increasing credit risk appetite on the part of the securities market because of the shortage of attractive assets to invest in, and downward pressure on real interest rates. These trends increase the danger that we can have debt-induced worldwide financial bubbles develop. Remember what is going on. Everyone is adding debt, including governments. As the ability of governments to control interest rates is eroded and you have a lot of people chasing a small supply of assets, there is a real potential for a securities boom and speculation to take over.

That is a quick overview of some of the forces at work in the economy. This should put securitization in perspective. It is a powerful trend, but it is not the only trend. It feeds and works with the other trends.

Let us think for a minute of what the banking and intermediation system is going to look like in the future. I believe there will be a large number of attractive roles. These include classic broad-based banks, global market makers in the wholesale markets, thousands of investor specialists, lots of disaggregated boutiques, as well as opportunities to find a utility or quasi-utility role like global custodians or rating agencies. There will also be roles in nearly any business for focused competitors who have either national- or global-class skills, whether they are delivering consumer finance or are making markets in derivatives.

Let us focus for a minute on one class of financial institution, the megabank. People find the concept of a megabank fascinating. Let us discuss what such an institution would look like. This beast, if it exists by the year 2000, will have $500 billion plus in assets. Most of those assets will not be in the bank though. They will be in a broad array of subsidiaries. We already have institutions approaching that size. Citibank/Citicorp already has $230 billion in assets, and Bank of America and Chemical Bank are at about $200 billion. Merrill Lynch will be of this size. The few institutions of this size that exist, maybe five or ten in the world, will exist because of synergy between the parts. There are considerable numbers of potential synergies justifying the existence of such institutions including taxes, funding, proprietary product, information, skill, and some shared distribution advantages. It remains to be seen if participants can actually capture these theoretical synergies. These institutions will not only be large, they will also be complex. Let me describe how a U.S. megabank might operate in a fully securitized, fully globalized world by describing how two of the major subsidiaries of such an institution might work. Let me call the first subsidiary a "core" bank. Let me call the second subsidiary a "global wholesale" bank.

The core bank, I believe, will be a firewall-separated, FDIC-insured, entity. These banks will probably have physical distribution in geographies with 50 percent of the population and will have nonphysical distribution to almost the entire country. The core bank subsidiary itself will probably have $300 billion in assets. Bank deposits keep going down, but the base is growing rapidly. If you only have 22 percent of the financial stock in a global capital marketplace with $80 trillion, you still have $22 trillion of assets in banks. Banks will not disappear because you will still have depositors, and if you have liabilities, you will still need assets. Seventy percent or more of the assets of the core bank will be in securities form. Core banks will also be major originators of securitized assets and mutual funds. The core bank will probably represent less than 50 percent of the holding company's assets, value added and capital. They will be distributors of loans, deposits, mutual funds, life insurance, annuities, property and casualty, and they will provide transaction services. If effective, they will be using multimedia and other channels of distribution. They will be segmenting by age, income, lifestyle, behavior, and so forth. They will use this information to produce information for investors, so you will be able to have some very specialized securities that will appeal to very specific investor classes. The core banks' profit leverage will come from their ability to understand and segment customers, from their ability to distribute, from the product value they add, from their skills in managing technology, from managing the costs of service delivery, and from management of core employees, contract labor, and funding. One of their most essential skills will be risk-return management. This is the management of portfolio credit risk and operations risk, and frontline credit-underwriting skills. They will be creative in offering products but will be skillful in disaggregating the embedded risks of those products and in getting rid of the risks they do not want to take and keeping the ones they do. These institutions will need global investment banking skills. One of the reasons you will find some institutions with both global investment banks and global retail banks is that the biggest client of the global investment bank will be the core bank attached to it. It is no coincidence that Nations Bank and Swiss Bank both acquired firms specializing in derivatives.

Another subsidiary of the megabank will be a global investment bank with $100 billion in assets. All of its assets will essentially be securities, 90 percent of its assets will be marked to market. The value added from this subsidiary from credit products will be as an originating structure, and from underwriting and trading credit risk, not from holding it. The global investment banks will largely be formed by merging existing wholesale banking departments with traditional investment banking firms.

Suggested Readings

Benston, G. 1992. "The Future of Asset Securitization: The Benefits and Costs of Breaking up the Bank." *Journal of Applied Corporate Finance* 5: 71–82.

Boemio, T., and G. Edwards, Jr. 1989. "Asset Securitization: A Supervisory Perspective." *Federal Reserve Bulletin* 75 (October): 659–669.

Bryan, L. 1989. "Introduction." *The Asset Securitization Handbook*. New York: Dow Jones Irwin.

Campbell, T., and W. Kracaw. 1993. "Securitization." *Financial Institutions and Capital Markets*. New York: Harper Collins.

Carron, A. 1992. "Understanding CMOs, REMICs and Other Mortgage Derivatives." *The Journal of Fixed Income* 2: 25–43.

Fabozzi, F., and F. Modigliani. 1992. *Mortgage and Mortgage-backed Securities Markets*. Boston: Harvard Business School Press.

Federal Home Loan Mortgage Corporation. *Secondary Mortgage Markets*. Quarterly.

Greenspan, A. 1995. Testimony Before Committee on Banking, Housing and Urban Affairs, U.S. Senate on Derivatives. *Federal Reserve System*, January 5.

Harvard Business Review. 1995. "Using Derivatives: What Senior Managers Must Know." *Harvard Business Review* 75: 33–42.

Jones, A., H. Hayssen, and J. Schneider. 1995. "Rating of Residential Mortgage-backed Securities." *The Journal of Fixed Income* 4: 12–36.

Kane, C., and S. Alpart. 1995. "The Emerging Market for Commercial Mortgage Conduits." *The Real Estate Finance Journal* 11: 35–46.

Kendall, L. 1995. "A Time for Retooling." *Mortgage Banking* 56: (forthcoming).

Lederman, J., ed. 1990. *The Handbook of Asset Backed Securities*. New York: New York Institute of Finance.

Norton, J., and P. Spellman, eds. 1991. *Asset Securitization: International Financial and Legal Perspectives*. Oxford, Cambridge MA: Basil Blackwell Finance.

Olasov, B. 1995. "The Maturing of the Commercial Mortgage-backed Securities Market." *Real Estate Review* 25: 10–15.

Saunders, A. 1994. "Securitization." *Financial Institutions Management.* New York: Dow Jones Irwin.

U.S. Congress, House Committee on Banking, Finance and Urban Affairs, Subcommittee on Policy Research and Insurance. 1991. *Hearing on Asset Securitization and Secondary Markets.* July 31.

U.S. Congress, House Committee on Banking, Finance and Urban Affairs, Subcommittee on Economic Growth and Credit Formation. 1993. *Hearings on Creation of Secondary Market for Commercial Business Loans.* March 2, 9, and 21, May 6.

Index